CW00338159

HOOD

LIFE AND DEATH OF A
BATTLECRUISER

ROGER CHESNEAU

HOOD

LIFE AND DEATH OF A BATTLECRUISER

CASSELL

To the memory of the sailors who gave their lives
in the Denmark Strait on Saturday 24 May 1941

CASSELL
Wellington House, 125 Strand, London WC2R 0BB

British Library Cataloguing-in-Publication data:
A catalogue record for this book is available from the
British Library.

ISBN 0-304-35980-7

Designed and typeset by the author

Printed and bound in Great Britain by Bath Press

Frontispiece: HMS *Hood* in mid-1932, at light displacement.

CONTENTS

PREFACE

FOR EIGHTY YEARS there has been a fascination about HMS *Hood*. She was, for two decades after her completion, the ultimate dreadnought—huge, graceful, fast, powerful, the epitome of naval might in the early years of the twentieth century. She left a lasting impression on all who saw her. This was the ship on which schoolboys with a leaning towards a career in the Royal Navy wished to serve; this was the ship the public wanted to see at Navy Days; this was the ship that sailed the world, a roving ambassador projecting Britain's military might in the way that US supercarriers do today; this was the ship

that everybody had heard of; this was the ship that potential enemies feared. When she was lost in May 1941 the news took on the proportions of a national tragedy: people gasped; people wept. Since her loss, the fascination has persisted, fuelled by the continuing discussion, often heated, about the reasons for her demise. Even with the recent discovery of her wreck—a brilliant feat of diligence, expertise and modern technology—few conclusions can be irrefutably drawn. The fascination will continue.

It is difficult to say when my own interest was sparked; certainly, I am of insufficient age to have had any first-hand knowledge of the ship. It probably came about when a kindly relative presented me with a prewar Players cigarette card album entitled *Modern Naval Craft*: card number 4 showed a picture of what was easily the most impressive vessel in the set. Some diligent schoolboy research revealed that card number 49 in the W. D. & H. O. Wills album entitled *Life in the Royal Navy* was an onboard view of the same ship. Then, in 1960, two things of significance happened: the film *Sink the Bismarck!* was released; and an Airfix kit of HMS *Hood* arrived on the shelves of the local Woolworths! One thing led to another: Ernle Bradford's book was borrowed from the local lending library and avidly devoured, old prewar copies of *Jane's Fighting Ships* were procured, further, more imaginative models were created from plastic kits, and, ultimately, many years later, a detailed model was produced which was—and may well still be—displayed in the National Maritime Museum in Greenwich.

A number of people gave willingly of their time and expertise in the preparation of this book, and I would like to thank them all profusely—in particular my friends John Roberts, Antony Preston and Paul Bevand. John loaned many of his valuable

Below: The origins of interest. *Author*

Above: The author's 1in:50ft scale model of HMS *Hood*, now with the National Maritime Museum, Greenwich. It features very fine non-proprietary guardrail and rigging detail. *Joananne Chesneau*

photographs, readily came up with advice relating to some of the finer points in the text and commented very constructively on the line drawings; Antony kindly read through the text and highlighted some modifications and additions that were called for; and Paul, in his capacity as administrator of the HMS *Hood* website, generously assisted with the provision of photographs and also read through, and commented upon, the text. I would also like to thank very much David Mearns, of Blue Water Recoveries, for kindly permitting me to reproduce photographs taken during the July 2001 expedition to locate and investigate *Hood*'s wreck; Gerhard Koop, Ian Johnston and Dick Cronin for their help with illustrations; and the staff at the Public Record Office in Kew. In addition, I am most grateful to Barry Holmes and George Sharp at Cassell, not only for their assistance and encouragement, but also for granting the rare privilege to an author of designing his own book.

Finally, a very personal note. My wife Joananne, as always, gave me her love, help and enthusiasm when I started out on this project, but, tragically, she did not live to see the end product. I hope very much that she would have liked it.

Roger Chesneau
Ringshall, Suffolk
February 2002

GENESIS

O N 20 MARCH 1908 a new type of fighting ship was completed for the Royal Navy. Named *Invincible*, she represented the latest thinking in armoured cruisers. She had evolved out of the fertile theories held by Admiral Sir John Fisher. In 1901, when he was Commander-in-Chief of the Mediterranean Fleet, Fisher had drawn up an idea for a novel variation, which, with characteristic flamboyance, he had named 'HMS Unapproachable'. Intended to surpass in quality existing foreign armoured cruisers, this ship was to be armed with a mixture of 10in and 7.5in guns (both of which could be hand-worked), to possess barely any superstructure save light bridgework, telescopic funnels and wireless aerials, and to be powered by turbine machinery driven by oil-fired boilers. Her speed of 25 knots would give her a decided edge over all contemporaries. Later modifications to these outline plans saw the main armament revised to 9.2in and 7.5in guns, disposed so as to permit the maximum possible ahead and astern fire, on a displacement of some 14–15,000 tons; the minimum length of the hull was envisaged as 500ft, with vertical armour protection up to a maximum of 6in over the most vital parts of the ship. Fisher's ideas were worked upon throughout 1902 and 1903, and in 1904 the final designs for the three-vessel *Minotaur* class were approved. The name ship was laid down at Devonport on 2 January 1905.

Designed by Philip Watts, the new cruisers did not quite match Fisher's expectations, but they went some way towards meeting them. They were in fact a refinement of the previous *Warrior* class, but the adoption of twin turrets for the larger main calibre permitted the disposition of ten 7.5in singles, giving a broadside of nine heavy weapons compared with six, and four ahead or astern compared with three, on a hull little

Below: The armoured cruiser *Achilles* of the *Warrior* class, direct predecessors of the *Minotaur*s. Armed with six 9.2in guns in single turrets and four 7.5in similarly mounted amidships, they were designed as much for battle fleet reconnaissance as for trade protection. *John Roberts Collection*

changed in general dimensions. The funnels, though squat, were of conventional form, and the superstructure was minimised. The ships made about 23 knots on trials and entered service in 1908–09. It escaped nobody's notice that the ships' armament approached the scale of that installed aboard the recently completed *Swiftsure* and *Triumph*, which were rated as second-class battleships, and that the *Minotaur*s, although more lightly armoured, were considerably faster than this pair.

On 20 October 1904—the eve of Trafalgar Day—Fisher took up his appointment as First Sea Lord and within two months had set up a Committee on Designs, which included among its number Sir Philip Watts, the Director of Naval Construction; W. H. Gard, the Chief Constructor at Portsmouth Dockyard; Rear-Admiral Sir John Durston, the Engineer-in-Chief of the Fleet; Captain John Jellicoe, the Director of Naval Ordnance; and Rear-Admiral Prince Louis of Battenberg, the Director of Naval Intelligence. Fisher himself took the chair. One of the early decisions reached by the Committee was to sanction the design process for what would become HMS *Dreadnought*, the world's first all-big-gun battleship, but it was not long before Fisher pressed his colleagues on the subject of the next evolution of the armoured cruiser. It was about this time—early 1905, just as the first *Minotaur*s were being laid down—that the Admiralty became aware of a significant development on the other side of the world: the Japanese were building armoured cruisers with four 12in and twelve 6in guns and a speed of 21 knots.

Below: *Invincible*, the first of the
battlecruisers. Her main armament
of 12in guns was disposed one twin
turret forward, one aft and two on
the beam amidships; the starboard
mounting of the latter pair can
readily be seen in this photograph.
The booms stowed along the hull
were for deploying anti-torpedo
netting when the ship was at
anchor. *John Roberts Collection*

Meanwhile the Italians, under their Chief Engineer Vittorio Cuniberti, were constructing fast battleships with a mix of 12in and 8in guns.[1]

It was not difficult to perceive in what direction the development of the armoured cruiser was proceeding: if an all-big-gun battleship was the pointer to the future, why not an all-big-gun armoured cruiser? The type's traditional roles —the defence of trade routes, and an ability to overcome equivalent foreign ships in this pursuit; reconnaissance for the Fleet; and 'showing the flag' in minor world troublespots— would not be compromised, but, armed with battleship-calibre guns, the ships could also form a 'fast wing' to the main battlefleet and contribute, perhaps decisively, in the context of a fleet action. In short, the type needed to be superior in speed and hitting power to the armoured cruisers of other navies.

The Committee on Designs considered five outline sketch designs for successors to the *Minotaur* class, all of about 17,000 tons and mounting either six or eight 12in guns in twin mountings disposed in various patterns but attempting to maximise ahead and broadside fire. The final decision was for an eight-gun ship with centreline turrets forward and aft and one each to port and starboard amidships, the latter pair mounted *en echelon* so that, in theory at least, in the event of one turret being disabled the other could fire across the deck and so maintain the weight of broadside.

Three ships with the agreed specifications—*Invincible, Inflexible* and *Indomitable*—were laid down in early 1906 and completed during 1908. Powered by turbine machinery fired by mixed coal and oil fuel, they were very fast vessels, reaching over 25 knots on trials and, unusually for warships, some 2–3 knots more in service. Their speed had, however, been purchased at a price: in broad figures, their vertical belt armour was only 6in maximum (compared with the contemporary *Dreadnought*'s 11in); their turret armour was 7in on the sides and faces and 2½in on the roofs (11in maximum); and they had ¾in armour on the main deck and a maximum of 2½in on the lower (¾in and 4in). Nevertheless, their armament was of a calibre capable of inflicting serious damage on enemy battleships, and critics foresaw the distinct possibility of the *Invincibles* being employed in the line of battle as well as in their cruiser roles—and the dangers to which they would be exposed as a result.

THE BATTLESHIP RACE

The early years of the twentieth century were characterised by German naval expansion, formulated by Admiral Alfred von Tirpitz, Secretary of the Navy, and given practical encouragement by the Kaiser, Wilhelm II. The principal goal of this expansion was an extension of German global influence, encompassing colonial prestige and increased seaborne trade to bolster the country's growing industrial might. The passing of Tirpitz's two Navy Laws, in 1898 and 1900, required the building of a fleet that would eventually number 38 battleships and eight large cruisers. The British, not unnaturally, saw this as a direct challenge to the pre-eminence of the Royal Navy. The advent of *Dreadnought* late in 1906, however, had the effect of wiping the slate clean in terms of battleship construction, for so radical was her layout and technology that all her predecessors appeared anachronistic by comparison. Her arrival spurred Germany on to even more ambitious schemes: an amendment in 1908 to the Second Navy Law required a building programme that would produce all-big-gun battleships in considerably greater numbers than the earlier Laws dictated, so much so that it was envisaged that, within ten years, the German Navy might well rival the Royal Navy in termsd of overall strength.

Armoured cruisers were included in the programme, and, just as *Dreadnought* provoked a direct response in the form of the *Nassau* class, so did *Invincible* prompt the Germans to build a reply. The ship concerned was *Von der Tann*, displacing 19,400 tons, armed with eight 11in guns and possessing a top speed of nearly 25 knots. Although the fact was played down in Admiralty circles at the time, she was also considerably better protected than the *Invincible*s, with 9½in of vertical armour over vital areas, broader in the beam and with superior underwater protection.

To the uninitiated—and to many who might have known better—Fisher's 'greyhounds of the sea' were the epitome of naval prowess, in the very best Nelsonian tradition, even if their precise role was never fully agreed upon. They were comely vessels, fast and powerful, and it was not long before more of the type were laid down. Within a year of *Invincible*'s completion, work on a lengthened edition, *Indefatigable*, had been begun, and she was joined in the summer of 1910 by two sister-ships funded by the Commonwealth of Australia and the Dominion of New Zealand and each carrying her country's name. The hull was lengthened slightly to enable the wing turrets to fire unimpeded across the deck, but the armour protection was on the same questionable scale. They were quickly followed by the very much bigger *Lion* class, and by the time these 26,000-ton, 660ft long, 13.5in-gun monsters were commissioned all pretence that these types of vessels were armoured cruisers had been abandoned and they were henceforth known as 'battlecruisers', the implication being, clearly, that they were front-line capital ships.

The German responses continued. *Von der Tann* was followed by the two ships of the *Moltke* class, with ten 11in guns on a displacement of 22,600 tons, and in turn by *Seydlitz*, an improved *Moltke*. Calibre was raised to 12in and wing turrets dispensed with in the three battlecruisers of the *Derfflinger* class. Meanwhile the type had also been adopted by the

Japanese, who placed an order with Vickers for a 26,000-ton battlecruiser, *Kongo*, in which the gun calibre was increased to 14in, with all four turrets mounted on the centreline as in *Lion* and *Derfflinger*; the Japanese themselves built three sister-ships.

Ninety years on, it is difficult to appreciate the depth of the rivalry between the major European powers—rivalry driven by fear, apprehension, indignation and (so each said of the other) aggression. Such was the intensity of the competition that, between the years 1907 and 1914, a new battleship or battlecruiser was being laid down, on average, every 3½ months in Germany and every 2½ months in Great Britain. The cost was enormous. Whether or not the war that began on 4 August 1914 was a direct outcome of that rivalry is arguable, but the conflict that raged over the next four and a quarter years would test the mettle of the fleets on a number of occasions. The building race continued too, though its pace slackened as funds were consumed by shifting priorities. The final entrant in that race was a battlecruiser named HMS *Hood*.

BATTLE

When war came, it was fully expected by both sides that a huge fleet action would take place in the North Sea at some point in the near future—a sort of modern-day Trafalgar—and that this might have a decisive effect on the outcome of the conflict as a whole. Things did not quite work out that way: the policy of the Royal Navy's Grand Fleet was to blockade the German High Seas Fleet and keep it bottled up in the North Sea, at the same time steering well clear of the traps that the Germans had set near their coast in the form of minefields and waiting submarines; and the Germans decided that they could not afford to risk losing a substantial portion of their fleet by committing it to combat and were content to wait behind their defences. Stalemate was rife.

Fleet action there may not have been, but skirmishes there were aplenty, and most of these involved the battlecruisers. Less than a month after the outbreak of war, on 28 August, British light forces became entangled with German cruisers in the Heligoland Bight and called upon Admiral Beatty's 1st

Above: *Lion*, along with her sister-ships *Queen Mary* and *Princess Royal*, made up the 'Splendid Cats'—three 27-knot, 13·5in-gun battlecruisers that, when commissioned, were the pride of the Navy The main armament was disposed all along the centreline, a single turret amidships being retained. *Lion* saw a good deal of action during the First World War; her sister *Queen Mary* was lost at Jutland as a result of a magazine explosion. *John Roberts Collection*

TABLE 1: PRINCIPAL CHARACTERISTICS OF FIRST WORLD WAR BATTLECRUISERS

Class	No of ships	Date	Displacement (tons)	Dimensions (length × beam × draught) (ft)	Armament Main	Secondary	Armour (in) Belt	Turrets	Deck	hp	Speed (kts)
British											
Invincible	3	1906	17,250	530 × 78.5 × 26.8	8 × 12in	16 × 4in	6	7	2½–1	41,000	25
Indefatigable	3	1909	18,500	555 × 80 × 27	8 × 12in	16 × 4in	6	7	2½–1	44,000	25
Lion	3	1909	26,270	660 × 88.5 × 28.75	8 × 13.5in	16 × 4in	9	9	2½–1	70,000	27
Tiger	1	1912	28,430	660 × 90.5 × 28.4	8 × 13.5in	12 × 6in	9	9	3–1	108,000	29
Renown	2	1915	27,950	750 × 90 × 27.5	6 × 15in	17 × 4in	6	11	3–1	112,000	30
Courageous	2	1915	18,600	735 × 81 × 23.3	4 × 15in	18 × 4in	3	13	1¾–¾	90,000	31
Furious	1	1915	19,513	750 × 88 × 24	2 × 18in	11 × 5.5in	3	13	1¾–¾	94,000	31.5
Hood	4	1916	36,300	810 × 104 × 29	8 × 15in	16 × 5.5in	9	15	3–1	144,000	32
German											
Von der Tann	1	1908	19,400	562.75 × 87 × 27.5	8 × 11in	10 × 5.9in	9½	9	2½	42,000	24.8
Moltke	2	1908	22,616	610 × 96.75 × 27	10 × 11in	12 × 5.9in	11	10	2½	52,000	25.5
Seydlitz	1	1911	24,610	656 × 93.5 × 27	10 × 11in	12 × 5.9in	11	10	2½	67,000	26.5
Derfflinger	3	1912	26,180	689 × 95 × 27.5	8 × 12in	12 × 5.9in	12	11	2½	63,000	26.5
Mackensen	4	1915	30,510	731.5 × 99.5 × 30.5	8 × 14in	15 × 5.9in	?	?	?	90,000	27
'Ersatz Yorck'	3	1916	33,000	747.4 × 99.5 × 30.5	8 × 15in	12 × 5.9in	11¾	10	3½	90,000	27.5

Dates are the years in which the vessels were laid down; displacement is normal displacement; dimensions are approximate figures; armour thicknesses are maximum figures; and speeds are designed speeds. Note the inexorable growth in ship size, power output, speed and armament, for both navies; and how, generally speaking, German battlecruisers had thicker vertical armour and a smaller-calibre main armament—though a heavier secondary armament—than their British contemporaries. However, contrary to much popular opinion, the horizontal armour of British battlecruisers did not compare unfavourably with that of the ships' German equivalents. *Courageous* and *Furious* were anomalies, mounting huge guns on a hull which barely compared with that of a light cruiser in terms of protection. Note also their shallow draught: they were envisaged by Fisher as operating in the Baltic, supporting an amphibious landing in Pomerania—a sort of 'second front'. In the event they proved to be an embarrassment to the Royal Navy, and after the war they were converted into fleet aircraft carriers, a role in which they were very successful. The data for *Hood* is that for the ship as originally designed.

Battle Cruiser Squadron for assistance. Beatty swept into action with *Lion*, *Princess Royal*, *Queen Mary*, *New Zealand* and *Invincible* and promptly blew three of the enemy vessels out of the water. *Invincible* was in the thick of things again a few months later, when, in company with her sister-ship *Inflexible*, she caught up with the German Pacific Squadron, comprising two armoured and three light cruisers, under Admiral von Spee off the Falkland Islands on 8 December. The German armoured cruisers, *Scharnhorst* and *Gneisenau*, took heavy punishment but eventually succumbed to the effects of almost 1,200 rounds of 12in shell fired at them. In neither of these actions was anything other than superficial damage sustained by the British battlecruisers—although their opponents had been somewhat inferior in speed and much more so in terms of hitting power.

The first occasion on which battlecruisers met each other on more or less equal terms was on 24 January 1915 when Beatty's Battle Cruiser Force—consisting of *Lion*, *Princess Royal* and *Tiger*, armed with 13.5in guns, and *New Zealand* and *Indomitable*, armed with 12in—deployed in response to the Admiralty's decoding of a German signal which indicated that Vice-Admiral Hipper's 1st Scouting Group was sallying into the North Sea in an attempt to engage any British light forces he might come across. Beatty sighted the enemy off the Dogger Bank early in the morning and gave chase. The German ships, comprising the 11in-gun battlecruisers *Seydlitz* and *Moltke*, the 12in-gun *Derfflinger* and the armoured cruiser *Blücher*, plus light cruisers, turned for home. As the battle unfolded, the hapless *Blücher* was smashed to a burning wreck as all the British ships, by dint of misinterpreted signalling, concentrated their fire on her.

The German battlecruisers, meanwhile, had given their full attention to *Lion*, the leading British ship, which during the course of the battle took a total of twelve hits, all of which inflicted serious damage. Her armour was pierced at the waterline forward, forcing one of her engines to be shut down and causing flooding, and another shell struck 'A' turret[2] magazine, which had to be flooded in order to extinguish the fire that had started there. *Lion*'s speed was reduced to 15 knots and she limped home, the last part of the voyage made under tow from *Indomitable*. In spite of official despatches to the contrary, the Battle of the Dogger Bank was not an auspicious event for the Royal Navy's battlecruisers. Very much worse was to follow.

Beatty and Hipper met again on 31 May 1916, but this time as the vanguards of their respective battle fleets. The previous day the Admiralty had decoded German wireless signals indicating that a sortie by the High Seas Fleet was imminent, and Admiral Jellicoe, the British Commander-in-Chief, had ordered his ships to sea in an attempt to intercept the Germans off the Skagerrak. A neutral merchant ship, investigated by both sides, was the unwitting catalyst to the greatest naval action of the war, although the battleships of each fleet—

unaware of each other's presence until the final moments—were hardly themselves engaged.

The battlecruisers, consisting of *Lion, Princess Royal, Queen Mary, Tiger, New Zealand* and *Indefatigable* on the British side and *Lützow, Derfflinger, Seydlitz, Moltke* and *Von der Tann* on the German, opened fire on each other at a range of 16,000yds. Fifteen minutes into the battle *Lützow* hit *Lion*'s 'Q' turret. The shell pierced the armour plating and exploded inside, killing the crew and starting a fire amongst the cordite charges. The cordite flashed downwards, but a split-second order by a mortally wounded officer[3] to close the magazine doors and flood the magazines saved Beatty's flagship from almost certain destruction. At 1603, three minutes later, *Von der Tann* landed two shells on and near *Indefatigable*'s forward turret and the British vessel vanished in a colossal explosion which killed 1,015 officers and men. At 1620 *Queen Mary* was hit, like *Lion*, on 'Q' turret. She had been under fire from *Seydlitz* but was now being targeted by *Derfflinger* as well, and at 1624 she was struck again, this time on the upper deck forward. There was an immediate explosion in 'Q' magazine and the battlecruiser disappeared in a huge pall of black smoke, taking with her over 1,200 officers and men.

The carnage was not over yet. At 1830 Rear-Admiral Sir Horace Hood, aboard *Invincible* and commanding the 3rd Battle Cruiser Squadron, which was attached to the Grand Fleet proper, gained contact with the German battlecruisers and,

Above: HMS *Queen Mary*, one of the Royal Navy's three 'Splendid Cats'—fast, heavily armed and very expensive, but vulnerable. *Author's collection*

sighting *Derfflinger*, exchanged fire. Within four minutes there was yet another searing explosion as *Invincible* was rent in two, her 'P' and 'Q' magazines amidships having gone up as a result of a hit on 'Q' turret. She lost over 1,000 of her complement. Hipper's ships did not emerge unscathed: *Lützow* managed to extricate herself but was so badly damaged that she had to be scuttled; *Seydlitz* was flooded with 5,000 tons of sea water and had to be beached; *Derfflinger* was also heavily damaged; and *Moltke* and *Von der Tann* were each hit four times though were repaired within ten weeks.

The fleet action proper never took place in any major way, being limited to brief skirmishes as Admiral Scheer, the German Commander-in-Chief, withdrew his ships, losing only one elderly battleship to torpedo fire.

LESSONS

The Battle of Jutland has been re-fought on paper countless times over the last eighty-odd years, particular attention being focused on the loss of the three British battlecruisers and why their fates contrasted so sharply with those of their German counterparts. From the point of view of the former, critics have

generally concerned themselves with three main topics: the thickness and quality of British armour plate; the composition and stability of the cordite used in the charges; and the arrangements within the turrets and beneath regarding ammunition handling.

While it was feared, even before Jutland, that the armour protection of British battlecruisers might be inadequate, it has to be remembered that the ships were not designed specifically to fight in the line of battle: their employment in such a role may have been inevitable given that competing navies were bound to match their capabilities with ships of their own, but it was not seen as a primary function. Furthermore, had they been armoured on the scale of a contemporary battleship, this could only have been achieved, on a hull of similar dimensions, by saving weight elsewhere, in other words at the price of speed or of a much reduced armament, thereby compromising their ability to catch and overwhelm enemy armoured cruisers (or battlecruisers). The charge is frequently levelled that it was the inadequacy of this armour that led to the loss of three of their number at Jutland.[4] However, it is by no means obvious that this is so. The common denominator amongst all three ships is that they were struck on main turrets immediately prior to the massive detonations which caused their loss, and while this may say something about the quality of the armour employed for the turrets it does not tell us much about the effectiveness of the armour employed elsewhere. The ranges at which the ships were struck are also of interest: 16,000yds in the case of *Indefatigable*, 14,500yds for *Queen Mary* and 10,000yds for *Invincible*. The maximum range of the German battlecruiser gun was, for all classes, some 21,000yds, and considering the angle of elevation of the barrels—no more than 22 degrees for *Derfflinger* and *Lützow*, 16 for the others—it is likely that the shells struck home at a relatively low angle of descent, penetrating vertical or near-vertical plate rather than horizontal: this is virtually certain in the case of *Invincible*; and *Tiger*, fighting just astern of *Queen Mary*, had her main belt penetrated at about the same range as her companion. Eyewitnesses to the actions all confirm a delay between the

TABLE 2: BRITISH BATTLECRUISER AND BATTLESHIP ARMOUR PROTECTION

Ship	Type	Year	Main belt	Bulk-heads	Bar-bettes	Turrets	CT	Upper deck	Main deck	Middle deck	Lower deck	Magazine screens
Dreadnought	Battleship	1905	11	8	11	11	11	–	¾	3	4	–
Invincible	Battlecruiser	1906	6	7	7	7	10	–	1	–	2½	2½
Neptune	Battleship	1909	10	8	9	11	11	–	1½	1¾	3	–
Indefatigable	Battlecruiser	1909	6	4	7	7	10	–	1	1	2½	–
Orion	Battleship	1910	12	10	10	11	11	–	1½	1	4	1¾
Lion	Battlecruiser	1909	9	4	9	9	10	1	–	–	2½	2½
Iron Duke	Battleship	1912	12	8	10	11	11	2	1½	1	2½	1½
Tiger	Battlecruiser	1912	9	4	9	9	10	1½	1	–	3	–
Hood	Battlecruiser	1916	12	5	12	15	11	1	3	–	2	–

Each battlecruiser (except *Hood*) is paired with its nearest contemporary battleship. Dates are the years in which the vessels were laid down; and armour thicknesses (quoted in inches) are maximum figures and are for general comparative purposes only. The distribution of armour and protective plating, particularly horizontal protection, was of course subject to variation and depended not only upon the disposition of the ship's vital areas (machinery, magazines, etc) but also upon the characteristics of the projectiles the protection was designed to defeat; for a particularly enlightening discussion of this topic, see N. Friedman, *Battleship Design and Development 1905–1945* (London, 1978). Nevertheless, the extent to which battlecruisers sacrificed armour is plain to see: speed was of the essence, a requirement not shared by battleships, which were expected to perform in concert in the line of battle and were thus in practical terms limited to the speed of the slowest ship in the line. Comparing *Dreadnought* and *Invincible*, the weight of armour accounted for 28 per cent of the total displacement in the former but only 19.5 per cent for the latter. However, note that *Hood*'s armour compares much more favourably with that of the battleships than with that of her predecessor battlecruisers. CT = conning tower.

shells bursting on board and the fatal explosions proper—30 seconds in the case of *Indefatigable*—which seems significant. This could be explained in terms of what is known to have happened on board *Lion*, and suggests that in all three instances the explosion was caused not by direct penetration of a magazine but by a chain reaction, with fire in the turret flashing downwards via the shell hoists and through open magazine doors, perhaps aided by liberties taken with regard to basic safety precautions. The stability of the cordite used in the charges for the shells has also been criticised: it was widely held that stored cordite, though it might burn, would not explode in the manner of old-fashioned gunpowder. This belief appears in retrospect to have been ill-founded.[5]

Measures were taken immediately after Jutland to address the shortcomings. In particular, anti-flash devices were introduced, magazine flooding arrangements were improved and safety routines were enhanced and rigorously practised. Despite the lack of direct evidence that horizontal protection was inadequate, additional armour was worked into the battle-cruisers' decks, especially over the magazines, and in some instances the main turret roofs were strengthened; typically, *Tiger* had an extra inch of armour fitted over her magazines and shell rooms and *Inflexible*, *Indomitable*, *Australia* and *New Zealand* another inch over the magazines and on the turret roofs.

Ships still under construction were similarly modified. Two new battlecruisers, *Renown* and *Repulse*, had been launched and were being fitted out even as Jutland was being fought. They were incredibly handsome ships, larger than anything yet built, mounting the latest 15in guns and capable of an astonishing 32 knots. Their protection, however, was on a scale little altered from that introduced for the *Indefatigable* class six years earlier. Additional armour plate was hurriedly worked into the ships above their magazines and on the turret roofs before trials were undertaken, during which *Renown* strained her hull. Their entry into service was received with much derision, their 'two rows of scuttles revealing for all to see the fact that they had only a thin strip of waterline armour',[6] and their frequent visits to the dockyard for modification led to their being dubbed 'Refit' and 'Repair'. Wartime action was limited to a brief skirmish on 27 November 1917 off the Heligoland Bight, when, in company with the very lightly armoured battle-cruisers *Courageous* and *Glorious* ('Outrageous' and 'Spurious' to the denigrators), *Repulse* met and exchanged fire with some German light forces in an inconclusive encounter.

The future for the battlecruiser was not bright. Found wanting at Jutland, criticised from all quarters for its vulnerability, hugely expensive to build and maintain and—with the gradual realisation that the High Seas Fleet was unlikely to sail again for a 'final showdown'—possibly even redundant, this class of warship was beginning even to have its *raison d'être* called into question. Moreover, Fisher, the creator and champion of the battlecruiser, had resigned his position as First Sea Lord in May 1915, and the driving force behind the building programme had therefore been lost. One last ship, however, would make its appearance—and it would be the largest warship the world had ever seen.

DESIGN

FIVE DAYS after *Renown* and *Repulse* were laid down, the keel was laid in Germany for the first of four ships of the *Mackensen* class, enlarged versions of the *Derfflinger* design but mounting 15in guns in place of the latter's 12in armament.[1] British intelligence became aware of the existence of this development about the summer of 1915, by which time two vessels, *Mackensen* and *Prinz Eitel Friedrich*, were on the stocks. The Admiralty felt obliged to respond, and in February 1916 the Director of Naval Construction was asked to prepare a series of designs for a battlecruiser with a speed in excess of 30 knots, carrying at least eight of the heaviest possible guns and an open battery of anti-torpedo weapons and with an armour protection scheme enhanced over that of existing battlecruisers. Within a few days outline specifications for six candidate ships had been prepared (Table 3). After some deliberation Design '3' was selected as the approved basis for the new class of battlecruiser, although for reasons which are unclear the Board of Admiralty specified a reduction in power from 160,000 to 144,000shp and an increase in the secondary battery to sixteen guns. Final approval of the design was given on 7 April 1916, and within a week orders were placed with three yards, John Brown, Cammell Laird and Fairfield; the choice of builder for a fourth ship was deferred pending a decision on existing workloads.

HOOD: LIFE AND DEATH OF A BATTLECRUISER

TABLE 3: BATTLECRUISER DESIGNS, FEBRUARY 1916

Ship	Disp (tons)	Length (ft)		Beam (ft)	Draught (ft)		Armament			Armour	shp	Speed
		oa	pp		Load	Deep	Main	Secondary	T/tubes	belt (in)		(kts)
'1'	39,000	885	835	104	26	29.5	8 × 15in	12 × 5.5in	2	8	120,000	30
'2'	35,500	840	790	104	25	28.5	8 × 15in	12 × 5.5in	2	8	120,000	30.5
'3'	36,500	860	810	104	26	29.5	8 × 15in	12 × 5.5in	2	10	160,000	32
'4'	32,500	757	710	104	25	29	4 × 18in	12 × 5.5in	2	8	120,000	30
'5'	35,500	830	780	104	25	28.5	6 × 18in	12 × 5.5in	2	8	120,000	30.5
'6'	39,500	880	830	104	26	29.5	8 × 18in	12 × 5.5in	2	8	120,000	30

Length oa is length overall, the maximum linear dimension of the ship; length pp is length between perpendiculars, i.e. the distance between the point of intersection of the stem and the waterline at load (or standard) displacement and the rudder axis. These designs were prepared following a good deal of input from Admiral Jellicoe, the Grand Fleet's Commander-in-Chief, who rejected the Board of Admiralty's original proposals for a new class of shallow-draught battleships developed from the *Queen Elizabeth*s. Other characteristics recommended by the Admiral included a main armament elevating to 25° and preferably 30°, the installation of the secondary armament on the forecastle deck rather than in casemated positions one deck lower (so as to improve its workability), a reduction in the size of the larger internal compartments (to facilitate damage control), and the provision of single masts (to confuse enemy observers as to the course and speed of the ship). His proposals were, of course, formulated before the experiences of Jutland. The 18in gun was a new weapon, officially referred to as the '15in B' gun for security reasons; it was later installed in the light battlecruiser *Furious*.

Even as the Grand Fleet was under way in the North Sea to do battle with the High Seas Fleet, the first materials were being gather together at John Brown's yard on Clydeside for Ship No 460.[2] Work was to proceed at a leisurely pace: it was appreciated that the war might be over before the ship could be commissioned,[3] and labour was not to be diverted unduly from urgent projects nearing completion. However, work ceased almost immediately as the post-mortems into the disasters of 31 May got under way. Armour protection—particularly horizontal armour protection—was high on the list of topics under discussion.

ARMOUR

The function of armour protection was to safeguard the fighting capabilities of the ship, first to ensure that it could stay

Below: Early days in the building of Ship No 460 at John Brown's yard on Clydebank, autumn 1916. Towards the bow (left), some of the flat keel sections can be seen, the vertical keel members yet to be attached. *National Archives of Scotland, courtesy of Ian Johnston*

afloat in an engagement, secondly to preserve its motive power, and thirdly to keep its offensive weapons—especially its main armament—intact and usable. Logically, ships were armoured on a scale that would protect them from shells fired by vessels they might be expected to meet in action, which usually meant ships of their own kind. Thus 12in-gun battleships might be expected to have a 12in waterline belt, preventing the hull from being pierced at or near the waterline and protecting vital areas such as machinery and magazines; a 12in thick conning tower, ensuring as far as possible the safety of the main control position; and 12in armour to the main turret faces, protecting the ship's firepower (since the main armament might be expected to be trained on the enemy during an engagement, turret faces were accorded a higher priority than their sides or roofs). Considerations of weight generally prevented these

ideals from being reached, but most battleship designs strived for them.[4] The reason the early battlecruisers were viewed askance in some quarters was simply this: with armour thicknesses between 30 and 50 per cent less than those of contemporary battleships, yet armed with similar large-calibre weapons, they would be very vulnerable to penetration when fighting their own kind.

Vertical protection was very much more important than horizontal. Before the outbreak of war in 1914, gun actions were expected to be fought at ranges of about 10,000yds, below the capabilities of the guns themselves but reckoned to be the distance at which hits could be registered with reasonable regularity. Trajectories were therefore quite flat, even with guns elevated to their maximum angle (13.5° in early dreadnoughts and battlecruisers), and the chances of a dipping shell at the end of its trajectory striking the deck of a warship were considered to be low. Horizontal protection was of course provided, though there was no obvious classical scheme as there was with vertical armour. Most capital ships settled for a 'layered' system, designed not so much to prevent shells from penetrating the decks as to prevent debris from shells that had burst in the upperworks, or had penetrated the hull elsewhere above the vertical belt, from damaging the vitals below the water-line.[5]

It came as something of a shock to discover, at Dogger Bank in early 1915, that hitting ships at ranges of 18–20,000yds—almost the limit of the big guns' capabilities—was quite feasible; at

Below: Ship No 460 on the slipway. As clearly shown, the main armour belt has yet to be fitted. Discernible beneath the recess for the armour, left of centre of the picture, are the doors covering the starboard submerged torpedo tubes. *John Roberts Collection*

Jutland, too, gunfire at ranges in excess of 16,000yds proved all too effective. Thus the problem of the dipping shell—'plunging fire'—needed to be addressed. Committees were formed to look into the matter, and while it was acknowledged that the loss of three battlecruisers at Jutland could probably be ascribed to the flashing of cordite from the turret to the

magazine, direct penetration of the magazine could not at that stage be ruled out and therefore steps should be taken to strengthen the horizontal protection of battlecruisers both serving in the Fleet and under construction.

Accordingly, the new battlecruisers, three of which were at this time in embryonic form at their various builders' yards (one of the four had yet to be laid down), came under close scrutiny. The recommendations arrived swiftly, and the design was recast within weeks to accommodate additional armour protection, particularly in terms of the decks (Table 4). As a result, the weight of armour allocated to the ship rose

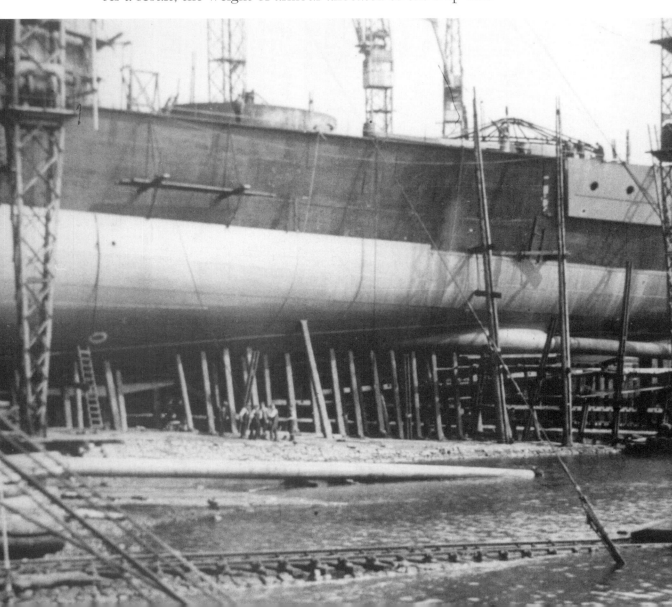

Below: Another view of *Hood* prior to her launching. The barbette for 'X' turret is clearly visible; that for 'Y' turret is less so. *John Roberts Collection*

from 10,100 tons (as of 31 May 1916) to 13,400 tons (1 September 1916), an increase of 32.6 per cent, and it rose again, albeit marginally, the following month when additional modifications were introduced. Displacement rose in sympathy, from 36,500 tons to 40,600 tons—a 14 per cent increase—and this had a serious effect on draught, which increased from 26ft to 27ft 9in forward and 28ft 9in aft at load (standard) displacement and from 29ft 6in to 31ft 6in (mean) in deep condition. Speed was expected to drop off by a knot as a result, but this was considered an acceptable price to pay for the increased protection.

ANTI-TORPEDO PROTECTION

In the years before and during the First World War, the danger to capital ships from enemy torpedoes occupied the minds of naval designers almost as much as that of shellfire.[6] The torpedo had demonstrated its potential in numerous encounters, particularly in the Japanese attack on Port Arthur in February 1904, and the prospect of swarms of torpedo-boats attacking capital ships *en masse*, or of lone submarines wreaking havoc among them, was taken very seriously indeed. Moreover, the necessarily short range of the torpedo was compatible with the ranges at which heavy ships were expected to engage each other.

The muzzle velocity of a typical First World War battleship or battlecruiser shell was of the order of 2,500 feet per second, say half a mile a second, or 1,800mph. Even allowing for the effects of friction and gravity as it travelled through the air, it still struck its target at a stupendous speed. The torpedo, by contrast, hummed through the water at

TABLE 4: MODIFICATIONS TO ARMOUR PROTECTION OF BATTLECRUISER DESIGN, 1916–17

	31 May 1916	1 Sept 1916	2 Oct 1916	30 Aug 1917
Vertical armour (in)				
Belt (forward)	5–4	7–6	7–6	6–5
Belt (amidships)	8–5–3	12–6	12–6	12–7–5
Belt (aft)	5–4	6	6	6
Bulkheads	4–3	6–4½	6–4½	5–4
Barbettes	9	12	12	12
Turrets (front)	11	15	15	15
Turrets (sides)	10	12	12	12–11
Turrets (rear)	10	12	12	11
Turrets (roof)	4¼	5	5	5
Conning tower	10	12	12	11–10–9–7
Torpedo control tower	6	6	6	6
Vertical protective plating (in)				
Torpedo bulkheads	1½–¾	1½–¾	1½–¾	1½–1–¾
Funnel uptakes	1½	2½	2½	2½–1½
Horizontal protective plating (in)				
Forecastle deck	1–1½	2–1¼	2–1¼	2–1¼
Upper deck	1–¾	1–¾	2–¾	2–1–¾
Main deck	1½	2–1½–1	3–1	3–2–1½–1
Lower deck (fwd)	2–1	2–1½–1	2–1½–1	1½–1
Lower deck (aft)	2½–1	2½–1	1½–1	3–1½–1

These figures show how the *Hood* design was modified over the months after she was originally laid down following the post-Jutland arguments; maximum and minimum values are indicated (very generally, the main belt thinned with distance both upwards from the waterline and towards the bows and stern, the conning tower as its walls descended into the bowels of the ship, and decks with distance from the magazines). Virtually the entire armour scheme of the ship was affected, but note particularly that the maximum thickness of the main belt was increased by 50 per cent and that the protective plating, especially over the magazines, was progressively increased (in fact, more or less doubled) during this time, so that, by the time she was completed, *Hood* had protection almost on a par with that of contemporary battleships.

Above: A view of the slipway, showing *Hood*'s massive propellers and rudder, the latter over 20ft wide at its broadest point. The pronounced bulging of the underwater portion of the hull amidships is evident. *John Roberts Collection*

perhaps 30 knots. Needless to say, the chances of a torpedo actually penetrating a ship's hull by virtue of its own motive energy were negligible: if it hit, it would explode against the outside, setting up enormous stresses, buckling plates and opening up gashes to admit inrushing water. Armour protection might help, but, for reasons of weight, it was impractical to armour the entire hull. Thus protection against the effects of an exploding torpedo concentrated on, first, dissipating the shock of the explosion as far as possible, then restricting the movement of any splinters that might be formed as hull plates

burst, and then confining flooding to as limited an area as possible.

Warship designers came up with many and varied answers to these problems. In the new battlecruisers, it was decided to bulge the underwater portion of the hull along the length of the main armour belt and divide it longitudinally into two sections, the outer containing plain air and the inner a mass of crushing tubes. The whole was divided laterally into a series of watertight compartments. The inner wall of the outermost section was composed of ½in plating and the inner wall of

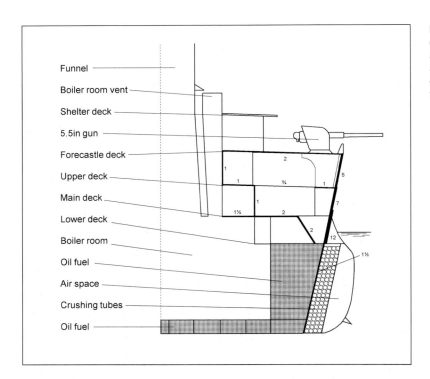

Funnel

Boiler room vent

Shelter deck

5.5in gun

Forecastle deck

Upper deck

Main deck

Lower deck

Boiler room

Oil fuel

Air space

Crushing tubes

Oil fuel

Left: A simplified transverse section of *Hood* taken approximately abreast the forefunnel, showing the anti-torpedo protection and the distribution of armour (with thicknesses in inches). *Author*

the innermost section, known as the torpedo bulkhead, comprised 1½in plating. The entire structure was held together by massive girders. Inboard again, and in effect part of the hull proper, were further compartments containing the bulk of the ship's oil fuel—again, self-evidently, watertight—backed by ¾in plating. Conveniently, and in keeping with conventional practice, these bunkers formed part of the overall scheme of anti-torpedo protection—a third layer of defence, as it were, against an explosion.

MACHINERY

Powerful machinery was required to drive the new battlecruiser through the water at over 30 knots, and the hull contained three enormous engine rooms, each 40ft long, two containing one Brown Curtis turbine set apiece and the forwardmost containing two side by side. Forward of the engine rooms were the four boiler rooms, each 40ft long also, their position within the hull betrayed by the huge twin funnels immediately above them. Each room contained half a

Right: A glimpse into one of *Hood*'s turbine rooms. Note the ship's badge. *HMS Hood Association/Ken Clark Collection*

dozen Yarrow oil-fired boilers working to 235psi. The boiler plant was complex, but in principle analogous to a modern oil-fired central heating system (though operating at vastly higher temperatures): each boiler was encased in tubes containing water, which, when heated to a sufficient temperature, would be converted to steam, which in turn could be led away to drive the turbine blades. Condensing plant reconverted spent steam into water, which was then recycled. For the first time in a capital ship, small-tube boilers were fitted in preference to large-tube: they were more compact

Above: Crewmen make
adjustments to the ship's
machinery. *HMS Hood Association/
Ken Clark Collection*

(though required more maintenance), saving weight and considerable space. The machinery rooms, in keeping with standard practice, were arranged along the centreline of the ship rather than side by side, which, it might be imagined, could have been more convenient for connecting the turbines to the ship's four propellers; in this way a centreline bulkhead was avoided, thereby ensuring that flooding, in the event of underwater damage to the hull, would be more evenly spread and the chances of a serious list minimised.

ARMAMENT

The new battlecruisers were to be fitted with eight 15in Mk I guns identical to those installed in the *Queen Elizabeth* and *Royal Sovereign* class battleships, the battlecruisers *Renown* and *Repulse* and the 'large light cruisers' *Courageous* and *Glorious*. After years of experimentation with wing turrets, wing turrets *en echelon* and single amidships turrets, designers had by 1916 long

Below: A simplified sectional drawing of *Hood*'s 15in 'Y' turret, showing the gun-loading arrangements and the positions of the magazines and shell rooms. Thicknesses of barbette and turret armour are indicated in inches. *Author*

Overleaf: *Hood* under construction, early 1918: a view looking forward from the stern. The 12in barbette armour for 'X' and 'Y' main turrets is prominent, and note also the thickness of the protective plating for the upper deck in the foreground. The line of the forecastle deck rising towards the prow can be distinguished. *Imperial War Museum*

settled on an all-centreline disposition, and, as in the *Queen Elizabeth*s and *Royal Sovereign*s, the new ships mounted two twin turrets forward and two aft, with 'B' and 'X' superfiring over 'A' and 'Y'. Four guns could therefore fire ahead and four astern, with the broadside eight on either beam. The guns were to be built by the Coventry Ordnance Works and Vickers, with those for the fourth ship at first undecided but later ordered from the builders, Armstrong Whitworth. Jellicoe's request in early 1916 for the elevation of the main armament to be increased was put into effect in the aftermath of the Battle of Jutland, and the original Mk I mounting was modified to permit an increase of 10° on the original 20°; for example, the working area at the breech had to be deepened to allow for its increased depression when the guns were fired at maximum elevation, although the maximum loading angle was still 20°. The modified mounting was known as the Mk II.

Each gun barrel was 54ft 2½in long, the bore length being 42 calibres or 52ft 6in; inclusive of its breech mechanism, it weighed a neat 100 tons. It fired an armour-piercing (AP) shell 5ft 5in in length or a high-explosive (HE) shell 5ft 7½in in

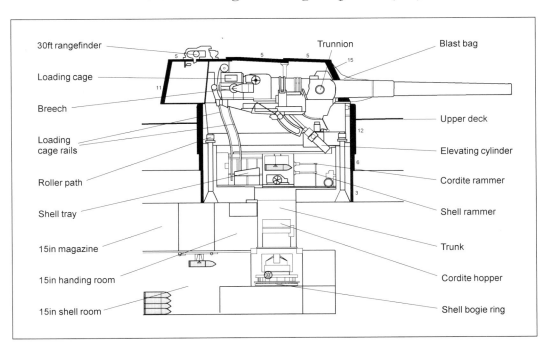

length weighing just over 1,900lb and requiring a charge of 428lb of cordite. The muzzle velocity of the gun was approximately 2,500fs and its theoretical maximum range (30° elevation) was 29,000yds (16½ miles); each gun could fire at the rate of one round every 30 seconds. The total weight of a 15in turret, with all its armour, was roughly 860 tons; hence a suite of 15in guns accounted for 3,440 tons, or some 8.5 per cent of the total displacement of the ships as originally designed.

The secondary armament was, as in the most recent battlecruisers, mounted high in the ships. It had been the practice with the latest battleships to mount the secondary battery in casemated positions at upper deck level, but experience showed that in any kind of seaway the weapons were notoriously difficult to work and the casemates flooded readily. The guns were arranged as twelve single mountings at forecastle deck level, six on either beam, two of which fired directly forward and one aft (all could be fired on the broadside); and four single mountings one deck higher on the shelter deck, one each forward and aft to port and starboard (and all capable of firing on the broadside). Each individual unit was protected by 1in shielding, and those guns on the forecastle deck[7] had

Right: *Hood* fitting out. The aftermost port 5.5in gun can be seen at left; the vacant embrasure further aft is where one of the four deleted mountings was to have been located. Three of the ship's four 4in AA guns can also be seen, the mountings covered by tarpaulins to protect them from the weather. On the hull, close to the 5.5in mounting, can be seen the twin doors for the port above-water torpedo tubes. *John Roberts Collection*

additional 1in plating fitted around their working spaces. The calibre selected was 5.5in, already earmarked for the light battlecruiser *Furious* and fitted also to the light cruisers *Chester* and *Birkenhead*. Its advantage over the standard 6in gun was that it had a longer range (18,500yds as against 13,500yds, thanks largely to the greater elevation provided by the mounting) and could be more easily hand-loaded. Before *Hood* was completed, and as a result of yet further modifications to the armour scheme, the four aftermost 5.5in guns were removed in order to save weight; thus the ship as completed could not bring its secondary armament to bear directly aft. The 5.5in Mk I gun was a 50-calibre weapon with an overall barrel length of 23ft 9in and a weight of 121cwt. It fired an 82lb shell using a 22¼lb charge of cordite and could elevate to 30°. The maximum rate of fire was 12 rounds per minute and its muzzle velocity was 2,725fs. It required a crew of nine men.[8]

In acknowledgement of the increasing danger of air attack on capital ships, a pair of 3in high-angle (HA) anti-aircraft guns were incorporated into the original design, but by the time the ships were laid down for a second time the AA suite had been amended to four 4in Mk V guns and these were what actually appeared on board *Hood*; two were sited on either side of the shelter deck just abaft the mainmast and two appeared at the extreme after end of the shelter deck arranged along the centreline. They were 45-calibre weapons weighing 43cwt, firing a 7¾lb projectile at 3,000fs to an extreme range of 13,000yds in the anti-surface mode (though considerably less in the HA mode).

Perhaps surprisingly, in view of the ranges at which actions involving big-gun ships were fought, the fitting of torpedo tubes in battleships and battlecruisers was the norm. The probability of making hits even at 10,000yds was unclear, but the torpedo was a potent weapon and fleet commanders were insistent that they be retained: a fleet of enemy battleships steaming close together in line of battle certainly made a tempting target. They were generally fitted below water, normally on the beam although it was increasingly the fashion to install one at the stern as well. The new battlecruisers omit-

Right: The bridge superstructure and, to the right of the photograph, the massive conning tower, surmounted by its 30ft rangefinder. Immediately below the rangefinder is the 15in gun control tower. The upper level of the conning tower proper was the main conning position and below this was the torpedo control, with viewing to port and starboard only; below this again were signals, intelligence and W/T offices. The whole structure was heavily armoured to resist hits by large-calibre shells. Range clocks are fitted adjacent to the torpedo look-out position on the foremast structure The forwardmost starboard 5.5in gun can be seen at the left; further aft, and one deck higher, can be seen the barrel of the shelter-deck mounting. *John Roberts Collection*

ted the stern tube but had one on either beam, piercing the bulge at its forward extremity, and the final (30 August 1917) design incorporated an additional eight fixed, above-water tubes, a pair on either beam at upper deck level abreast the after funnel and a further pair abreast the mainmast. The torpedoes shipped were the standard 21in type.

Four 3pdr Hotchkiss saluting guns were also to be carried, mounted in pairs to port and starboard on the Admiral's signal platform on the bridge super-structure.

FIRE CONTROL

Hitting a moving target at sea is no easy matter, and as battle ranges opened up during the early years of the twentieth century it became more and more diffi-cult, especially in any kind of seaway. As ranges increased, the problem of scoring hits became less and less a question of striking the sides of the target as one of landing shells on top of it (hence the pre-occupation, post-Jutland, with horizon-tal armour). The distance at which a target was to be fired at was calculated by means of a rangefinder, usually of the coincidence type in the Royal Navy: an observer saw two images in the viewer, and when these lay one on the other (i.e. coincided) the range could be read off.

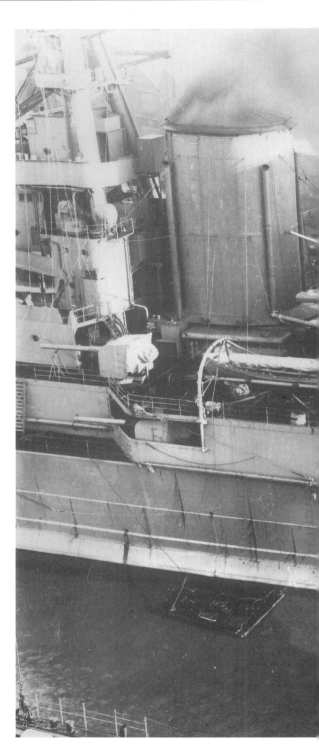

Right: Amidships, port side, showing the two huge funnels, details of the boat stowage and the disposition of the midships secondary battery. Note the searchlight platform between the funnels, the torpedo control tower with 15ft rangefinder abreast the platform and the 40ft derrick abaft this. *John Roberts Collection*

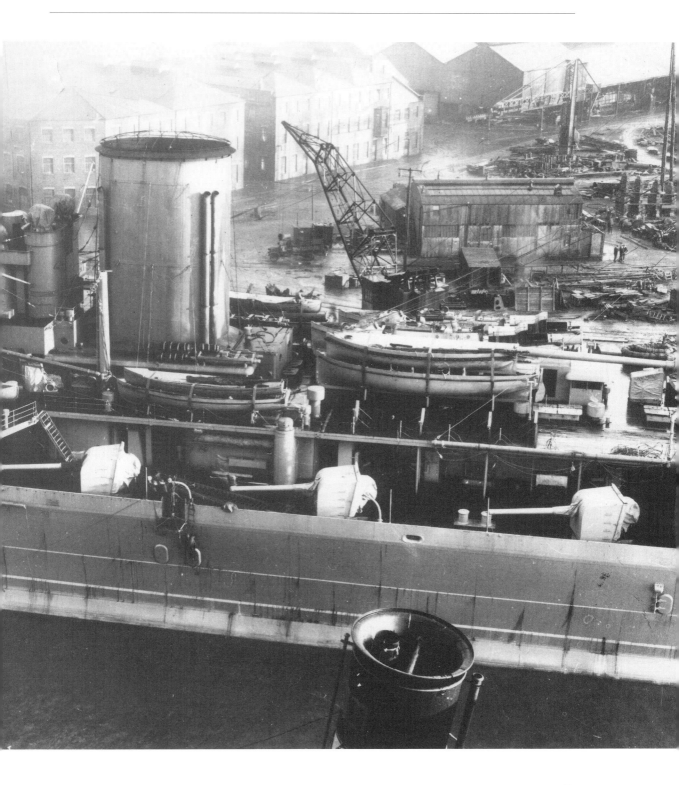

Rangefinders were fitted on the gun turrets, but from 1912 also elsewhere in the ship, as high as possible so as to view the target more clearly and also lessen any interference from smoke belching from the gun barrels. Once the range was found, the guns were fired and the splashes made by the shells were observed (again, these could be viewed all the more clearly from a position high in the ship); any necessary corrections to the aim were calculated, and a second salvo would be on its way.

It was not long before 'director firing' was introduced: all the gunlaying was conducted and all the required corrections worked out in one place—indeed, the guns could actually be fired from that same position as well, with predictions calculated for moving targets and the delay necessary to ensure that firing took place at the precise moment the ship was on an even keel all taken into consideration.

Each turret making up the main armament of the new battlecruisers was equipped with a 30ft rangefinder, to be utilised generally for local control (i.e. if the main director was rendered inoperable for any reason). An armoured conning tower, sited immediately abaft 'B' turret and before the bridge, carried a further 30ft rangefinder, its vitals enclosed in an armoured hood. High up on the foretop, above the bridge, a 15ft rangefinder was also protected by a hood. The secondary 5.5in guns were controlled from a platform below the main control position, with 9ft rangefinders to port and starboard in the foretop; director towers for these guns were situated on either side of the bridge. For AA control, a 2m rangefinder was sited on the after control position towards the after end of the shelter deck, close to the weapons themselves. A torpedo lookout position was located on the foremast, beneath the foretop proper and above a searchlight platform, and control positions were located within the conning tower forward, to port and starboard abreast and between the funnels, and right aft on the shelter deck; those amidships and aft were equipped with 15ft rangefinders, and that on the after torpedo control position was shielded by an armoured hood.

The main conning tower itself was a massive and complex structure and consumed well over 600 tons of the ships' weight. It contained not only the conning position proper, but also gun and torpedo control positions, intelligence offices, signals offices and wireless transmitting stations—in short, all the crew and equipment necessary for the strategic operation of the ships. Along with the main belt, turrets and barbettes, it was the most heavily armoured part of the design.

Searchlights were distributed as follows: four on a tower between the funnels (36in), two on the after control position

Above: Amidships, starboard side. The mainmast and its 65ft derrick can be seen at left, and in the foregound at left is one of the ship's four 4in HA guns. Note the 40ft derrick stowed above the aftermost 5.5in gun and the Carley liferafts nearby. *John Roberts Collection*

(36in), two on a platform on the foremast (30in) and two on the wings of the Admiral's bridge (24in).

FURTHER MODIFICATIONS

During their construction, warships may be subjected to all sorts of design modifications as influential persons recommend changes in the light of evolving technology or the experience of actual engagements. The new battlecruisers were designed in a world at war; and, as we have noted, the results of the Battle of Jutland had a major impact on their detail form. Ships are particularly vulnerable to 'tinkering' if their building schedules are relaxed, as was stipulated when the orders for the new ships were approved on 13 April 1916, and piecemeal modifications continued throughout the period of construction.

The new battlecruisers were allocated names on 14 July 1916; those selected recalled famous admirals of days gone by. However, eight months later work on *Howe*, *Rodney* and *Anson* was slowed almost to a standstill when the Admiralty communicated to the builders that all other work at the yards was to

Below: Port side, forward: another photograph of *Hood* fitting out, with the armoured hoods of 'A' and 'B' turrets yet to be cpmpleted. *National Archives of Scotland, courtesy of Ian Johnston*

TABLE 5: SHIPS OF THE *HOOD* CLASS

Name	Builder	Ordered	Laid down (i)	Laid down (ii)	Launched	Completed	Commissioned
Hood	John Brown, Clydebank	19 Apr 1916	31 May 1916 ?	1 Sept 1916	22 Aug 1918	5 Mar 1920	29 Mar 1920
Howe	Cammell Laird, Birkenhead	19 Apr 1916	31 May 1916 ?	16 Oct 1916	–	–	–
Rodney	Fairfield, Govan	19 Apr 1916	31 May 1916 ?	9 Oct 1916	–	–	–
Anson	Armstrong Whitworth, Elswick	13 Jun 1916	Jul 1916 ?	9 Nov 1916	–	–	–

The two dates for keel-laying are explained by the fact that work was temporarily suspended after Jutland while the design was re-cast; however, see Note 2 for this Chapter. The ships' names were allocated on 14 July 1916. Work on *Hood's* three sister-ships was suspended on 9 March 1917 and the projects were formally cancelled in November 1918; the relatively paltry sum of £860,000 had been spent on all three—an indication of the relaxed building schedule that had been followed.

take precedence, including the construction of merchant ship-ping.

On 6 March 1917 the Director of Naval Ordnance drew the Admiralty's attention to the relative positions of the forward 15in and 5.5in shell rooms and magazines. The latter were sited directly over the former, and he felt that, as a precaution against plunging fire, the positions should be reversed. His concern over the after magazines was less intense, as he believed that the danger from an exploding mine was greater than that from plunging fire along the after half the ship and so the magazines should be sited as far as possible from the keel.[9] He also recommended that the layout of the conning tower should be re-thought, advising that the various stations be taken lower into the hull. Some exchanging of positions within the conning tower did take place, but by this time work on Ship No 460 had advanced to the point where it was too late to make wholesale alterations, although the DNO was informed that his misgivings would be addressed in the three sister-ships.

Three months later Admiral Sir David Beatty, who had led the Battle Cruiser Force at Jutland and was now Commander-in-Chief of the Grand Fleet, complained about the armour plate on the main turret roofs, and requested that this be increased to 6in. He wrote again to the Admiralty in September 1917 questioning various aspects of the ships' design, including the detail layout of the bridge superstructure, what he considered to be poor subdivision of the machinery spaces, and the fact that the amidships 5.5in guns had no overhead

TABLE 6: RESULTS OF INCLINING EXPERIMENTS, ROSYTH, 1920

| | Design 31 May 1916 | | | Design 30 Aug 1917 | | | Inclining trials 21 Feb 1920 | | |
	Light	Load	Deep	Light	Load	Deep	Light	Load	Deep
Displacement (tons)	–	36,500	–	–	41,200	–	41,000	42,670	46,680
Mean draught (ft-in)	–	26-0	29-6	–	28-6	31-6	28-3	29-3	32-0
GM (ft)	–	–	–	–	3.3	–	3.2	3.25	4.2
Freeboard (forward, ft-in)	–	32-0	–	–	29-0	–	–	29-0	–
(amidships, ft-in)	–	23-6	–	–	21-11	–	–	21-0	–
(aft, ft-in)	–	19-0	–	–	18-9	–	–	17-0	–

Mean draught is an average of forward and aft values. Freeboard is the vertical distance between the waterline and the edge of the weather deck. GM is metacentric height. Put simply, this is the distance between the ship's centre of gravity (G) and its metacentre (M), the point at which an imaginary line drawn through the centreline of the ship upwards from point G intersects with a second imaginary perpendicular line drawn upwards from the centre of buoyancy, or the centre of gravity of the underwater portion of the ship's hull (B). Crudely, G is a downward pressure and B an upward pressure; and B will shift, depending upon the ship's angle of roll. The lower the GM, the more stable the ship (and the better gun platform she therefore makes), but stability may of course be disturbed by battle damage, especially as this will tend to affect one side of the ship only. The progressive increase in displacement can be explained almost entirely by the additional protection worked into the design as building progressed, leading inevitably to increases in draught and consequent reductions in freeboard.

protection for the gun crews. Most of his criticisms were rejected as being too costly (in terms of weight) or otherwise inexpedient, although he was informed that much of what he advocated could be incorporated into the three ships whose building schedules had slackened. Beatty would not give up, and in July 1918 he approached the Admiralty again, this time with his views concerning the disposition of the magazines and shell rooms in *Howe*, *Rodney* and *Anson* and requesting that additional protective plating be fitted over the main magazines in all four ships. This time his ideas were addressed more to his satisfaction, although by now it was evident that the ships might never be completed. In the first ship, however, the plating over the magazines was increased from 1in to 2in, and in compensation that around the base of the funnels was removed.

More modifications were made to the armour scheme when in May the following year, following firing trials against mock-ups, it was agreed that 3in protection should be added to the sides of the main deck over the main magazines; it was this additional weight that forced the deletion of the four aftermost 5.5in guns, thereby reducing the secondary battery to twelve mountings. In July 1919 still further changes were proposed— the main-deck protective plating over the magazines was to be increased yet again, to a total of 5in forward and 6in aft—and in anticipation of these the four torpedo tubes abreast the after funnel were removed and their ports plated over, the armoured casings of the four tubes abreast the mainmast were deleted and the after torpedo control position had its 6in armour replaced by 1½in plating. It was anticipated that the four above-water tubes that remained would be temporary fixtures only, to be removed once peacetime trials had been conducted, but in the event they stayed.[10]

Another modification concerned the tripod mainmast, the principal function of which was service as a derrick post for general duties, including the handling of the ship's boats; this had been a feature of earlier capital ships, such as the *Iron Duke* class battleships and the battlecruiser *Tiger*. However, early in 1919 it was decided to fit a main topmast and topgallant mast.

COMPLETION AND TRIALS

HMS *Hood* was launched at John Brown's yard on Clydebank on 22 August 1918, at 860ft 7in the longest warship to have been built for the Royal Navy—a distinction she holds to this day. The ceremony was performed by Lady Hood, widow of Sir Horace Hood who had perished aboard *Invincible* on 31 May 1916.[11] The launch weight was 21,920 tons. The ship then proceeded to fitting-out, to have her turbines, armament and superstructure installed, together with the main belt armour and the myriad items of minor equipment necessary to take her to the stage where she could leave for Rosyth, where final completion was to take place. Meanwhile, in November 1918, the contracts for her three sister-ships were finally cancelled.[12] The war had finished, and no rival ships were in prospect; moreover, the design had been so complicated by piecemeal adjustments that a fresh start was considered necessary.

Hood left John Brown's yard on 12 January 1920 on the northabout route and her behaviour in a seaway could be monitored for the first time. She ran preliminary sea trials in the North Channel, where the major concerns were that, even at comparatively light condition (she was drawing 29ft 10in mean) and in a Force 8 wind, she took a lot of water over the foredeck and her quarterdeck was awash, and that at 28 knots the spotting top vibrated excessively.

On reaching Rosyth two days later *Hood* was prepared for inclining experiments to assess her stability and calculate her true displacement; these took place on 21 February 1920. It was of course already understood that her displacement would exceed that of the 'final' design of April 1916, but the tests showed that she was some way over even the revised figure.

Below: *Hood* at speed early in her career, her main turrets and director control towers trained to starboard. *Bibliothek für Zeitgeschichte*

Sea trials took place the following month, for which *Hood* returned to the Firth of Clyde. Steaming back and forth over the measured mile off Arran, she worked up to 32.07 knots at load displacement (42,400 tons), at an output of 151,280shp; at deep displacement (44,600 tons) the figures were little changed—31.89 knots at 150,220shp. Her machinery functioned perfectly, and the figures exceeded the designed 31 knots at 144,000shp. Later in March gunnery trials were conducted, all the armament from the 15in guns down to the saluting guns on the bridge being exercised. These trials were also satisfactory, apart from some minor technical deficiencies with the main armament and, inevitably, some blast damage. The ship then sailed for Clydeside, where her builders completed their work, and in May *Hood* went once more to Rosyth for a thorough inspection. On 29 March 1920 she was commissioned into Royal Navy service—the largest, and by general agreement the most fetching, warship to hoist the White Ensign. She had cost around £6 million.

PEACE

IMMEDIATELY upon commissioning *Hood* departed for Plymouth, commanded by Captain Wilfred Tomkinson and crewed by some 1,400 officers and men, many of whom had been drawn *en masse* from the battlecruiser *Lion*, one of *Hood*'s predecessors, veteran of Dogger Bank and Jutland and one-time flagship of the 1st Battle Cruiser Squadron. Tomkinson had in fact been aboard during her trials, but the ship's first admiral, Sir Roger Keyes, did not join her until she arrived at Devonport, hoisting his flag on 18 May 1920. *Hood* was now officially flagship of the Battle Cruiser Squadron, which comprised, besides her, *Repulse*, *Renown* and *Tiger*.

The ship was quickly into her duties. Keyes had been ordered to take *Hood*, *Tiger* and a handful of destroyers and conduct some gunboat diplomacy off the coast of Estonia, as a show of strength in pursuance of the British Government's policy of opposing the Bolshevik 'Red' Army, although by this time 'White' Russian forces had virtually disintegrated and British troops in outposts

Below: *Hood* in the latter half of 1921, with plenty of spray drenching the forecastle. *John Roberts Collection*

56

such as Archangel, Baku and Murmansk had long since been recalled. The ship was readied at Devonport and sailed on 26 May. The cover story for the benefit of the crew was that *Hood* was en route to Scandinavia for a goodwill visit, and, having called at Scapa Flow, she duly anchored off Kristiania (Oslo) on 1 June. Here she was visited by King Haakon and Queen Maud (the sister of George V) and a host of dignitaries. The next port of call was Kalmar in Sweden, then Nynäshamn, just south of Stockholm, where further VIPs were conducted aboard. On 15 June *Hood* visited Danish waters, calling at Apenrade (Åbenrå or Aabenraa) to mark the recovery of Slesvig from German occupation, and on the 18th she navigated the Danish islands to the westward, arriving in Copenhagen the following day. Here she was visited by further guests, including King Kristian. She did not proceed to Reval in Estonia as planned owing to a change of mind by the Government, but sailed for home, calling again at Kristiania and hosting King Haakon for the second time in a month.

The new battlecruiser continued her shake-down cruises in home waters throughout the summer and autumn of 1920

and from 6 December until 6 January 1921 was docked at Devonport for a minor refit. Modifications were made to her bridgework, and the after searchlight platform was altered to include a control position. It was probably at this time that launching platforms for light aircraft were added on top of 'B' and 'X' turrets. By the end of the First World it had become

Right, upper: *Hood* in 1921 or 1922. The four searchlights originally positioned between the funnels have been reduced to two. *John Roberts Collection*

Right, lower: *Hood* as flagship of the 1st Battle Cruiser Squadron, Atlantic Fleet, in the early 1920s. *John Roberts Collection*

TABLE 7: PRINCIPAL PARTICULARS OF *HOOD*, 1920

Displacement		41,125 tons light; 42,670 tons standard; 46,680 tons deep
Dimensions	Length	810ft 5in pp; 850ft 7in wl; 860ft 7in oa
	Beam	104ft 2in max
	Draught	27ft 11in forward, 30ft 7in aft; 32ft 0in mean deep
	GM	3.2ft light; 4.2ft deep
Machinery	Boilers	24 Yarrow small-tube
	Turbines	Brown Curtis single-reduction geared
	Shafts	Four
	Shaft horsepower	144,000
	Max speed	31kts
	Endurance	7,500nm at 14kts
Bunkerage	Oil	3,900 tons normal
	Coal	58 tons
Armament	Main	Eight 15in 42cal Mk I on twin mountings Mk II; max stowage 120 rounds/gun
	Secondary	Twelve 5.5in 50cal Mk I on single mountings CP Mk II; max stowage 200 rounds/gun
	Anti-aircraft	Four 4in QF Mk V on single mountings HA Mk III; max stowage 150 rounds/gun
	Saluting	Four 3pdr Hotchkiss on single mountings Mk I; max stowage 64 rounds/gun
	Torpedo tubes	Two 21in submerged; four 21in above-water
Armour	Belt	12in–7in–5in amidships; 6in–5in forward; 6in aft
	Bulkheads	5in–4in
	Barbettes	12in–3in
	Turrets	15in front; 12in–11in sides; 11in rear; 5in roof
	Conning tower	11in–3in; 6in–3in–2in director hood; 3in tube
	Torpedo conning tower	3in–1½in; 4in–3in director hood; ¾in tube
Protective plating	Forecastle deck	1½in over magazines, 2in– 1¼in amidships
	Upper deck	2in over magazines; 1in–¾in amidships and aft
	Main deck	3in over magazines; 2in–1½in amidships; 1in forward; 2in aft; 2in slope
	Lower deck	1in forward; 1½in over torpedo rooms; 2in over magazines; 1½in–1in aft; 3in over steering gear
Complement		1,397

TABLE 8: ADMIRALS AND CAPTAINS ABOARD HMS *HOOD*, 1920–1941

Admirals		Captains	
May 1920–Mar 1921	Rear-Admiral Sir Roger Keyes	Jan 1920–Mar 1921	Captain Wilfred Tomkinson
Mar 1921–May 1923	Rear-Admiral Sir Walter Cowan	Mar 1921–May 1923	Captain Geoffrey Mackworth
May 1923–Apr 1925	Rear-Admiral Sir Frederick Field	May 1923–Apr 1925	Captain John K. im Thurn
Apr 1925–Jan 1928	Rear Admiral Sir Cyril Fuller	Apr 1925–May 1927	Captain H. O. Reinold
Aug 1928–Apr 1929	Rear-Admiral Sir Fredeck Dreyer	May 1927–May 1929	Captain Wilfred French
June 1929–May 1931	*Ship in refit (Portsmouth)*	June 1929–May 1931	*Ship in refit (Portsmouth)*
July 1931–Aug 1932	Rear-Admiral Wilfred Tomkinson	May 1931–Aug 1932	Captain J. F. C. Patterson
Aug 1932–Aug 1934	Vice-Admiral Sir William James	Aug 1932–Aug 1933	Captain Thomas H. Binney
Aug 1934–Jul 1936	Vice-Admiral Sir Sidney Bailey	Aug 1933–Nov 1935	Captain F. J. B. Tower
Nov 1936–Jul 1937	Vice-Admiral Sir Geoffrey Blake	Nov 1935–Aug 1937	Captain Arthur F. Pridham
Jul 1937–Aug 1938	Vice-Admiral Sir Andrew Cunningham	Aug 1937–Jan 1939	Captain Harold T. C. Walker
Aug 1938–Aug 1939	Vice-Admiral Geoffrey Layton	May 1939–Feb 1941	Captain Irvine G. Glennie
Aug 1939–Mar 1940	Vice-Admiral William J. Whitworth	Feb–May 1941	Captain Ralph Kerr
Jun–Aug 1940	Vice-Admiral Sir James Somerville		
Aug 1940–May 1941	Vice-Admiral William J. Whitworth		
May 1941	Vice-Admiral Lancelot E. Holland		

Note that, for the ship's first commissions, *Hood*'s admiral 'brought with him' a new captain. This practice was discontinued in the mid-1930s.

---

the practice within the Fleet to equip capital ships—and some cruisers—with aircraft in this way, to provide a defence against high-flying Zeppelins and also to spot for the fall of shot during an engagement. Positioning the runways on the tops of main turrets ensured that the equipment was kept well out of the way of discharging guns and also enabled the aircraft to be turned into the wind for launching, thereby shortening their take-off runs. However, at this time there were no means of recovering the aircraft once the latter were in the air: pilots had to try to make the nearest landfall or, more likely, ditch in the sea.

Below: *Hood* after her 1923 refit but prior to departing on the World Cruise. Awnings are rigged amidships and aft. The function of the fitting sited on the after searchlight platform, abaft the searchlights themselves, is uncertain but is believed to be a W/T tower. A main topgallant mast would be shipped prior to the ship's departure on the Cruise. *John Roberts Collection*

On 19 January 1921 *Hood* sailed south, again in company with *Tiger* and destroyers, on a 'Spring Cruise' to Gibraltar, calling at Arosa Bay and Vigo in north-west Spain en route. A few hours out from Torbay, where the squadron had ridden out a storm prior to their departure, news was received that the submarine *K5*, which had been accompanying the big ships, had gone down with all hands. *Hood* and her companions stood ready to assist, but in the event they were not required. By the end of March *Hood* was back at Devonport and Keyes and Tomkinson had stepped down, their places taken by Rear-Admiral Sir Walter Cowan and Captain Geoffrey Mackworth.

WASHINGTON

The end of the Great War in 1918 saw a defeated Germany and brought about the end of the 'battleship race' that had preceded it and had continued, though at a less furious pace, during the years of conflict. However, the dangers of a new rivalry were perceived, this time involving Great Britain, the United States and Japan, all of whom were pursuing building programmes to create ever larger battleships and battle-cruisers.[1] At the instigation of the United States, a conference was called in Washington in the summer of 1921 and delegates from Great Britain, the US, Japan, France and Italy convened on 21 November. Feelings were mixed, but a powerful opening speech by the US President, Warren Harding, laid the groundwork for some hard bargaining and by 6 February 1922 agreement had been reached. Briefly, Britain was to retain 580,000 tons of capital ships, the US 500,000, Japan 301,000, France 221,000 and Italy 182,000; gun calibres were to be limited to 16in and individual displacements to 35,000 tons; no new building was to be commenced for ten years (although Britain could build two new ships since, unlike the US and Japan, she had no 16in-gun ships in service[2]), and capital ships were not to be replaced until they were twenty years old; and modifications to ships in service were to be limited to strengthening their defences against air and submarine attack and in any case should not add more than 3,000 tons to existing individual displacements. In terms of numbers of ships, Britain could re-

tain 22, the United States 18 and the other three powers ten each. Since the Royal Navy at the end of 1921 had in service over forty battleships and battlecruisers, wholesale scrapping would have to take place, as indeed it would need to in the rival navies, much of whose new construction was broken up on the slipways.

Hood stood aloof from all this and continued to go about her business. She had undergone a short refit at Rosyth dockyard in June and July 1921 for alterations to the roof of her forebridge, to permit the installation of an 8ft rangefinder, and modifications to her complement of searchlights. In March 1922 she left for another 'Spring Cruise', this time taking in Gibraltar; Malaga and Alicante in southern Spain; Toulon, renowned for its status as the home port for the French Mediterranean Fleet; and, on the homeward leg, Vigo. Throughout the duration of these cruises, every opportunity was taken to carry out drills, trials and exercises both to test new tactics and to maintain and improve crew efficiency. Sometimes these exercises were conducted with other ships: for example, during the 1922 Spring Cruise the battlecruisers *Renown* and *Repulse* and the battleships *Valiant* and *Warspite* joined with *Hood* on a number of occasions.

Left: *Hood* at peace, with awnings raised. This photograph dates from the early 1920s; it was probably taken around the time of the World Cruise, since the main topgallant mast, carrying W/T yards, is rigged. The aircraft take-off platform stowed on the roof of 'X' turret is visible. *US Naval Historical Center*

The ship was back in home waters on 10 April 1922 and remained there until mid-August, when she sailed again for Gibraltar. During this time the usual round of exercises took
place, including torpedo trials, gunnery practice and inclination tests. On 5 July HM King George V came aboard and
carried out an inspection. *Hood*'s companion for the Gibraltar
cruise was *Repulse*, and at the end of the visit, on 20 August,
the two battlecruisers departed for the West Indies and South
America, the primary purpose of the voyage being a presence
at Rio de Janeiro to take part in the celebrations marking the
centenary of Brazilian independence. En route the ships called
at St Vincent. The visit to Brazil lasted throughout September
and was marked by the usual round of 21-gun salutes, em-
barking dignitaries, march-pasts and sporting events, and at
its conclusion the two ships left for Trinidad, Barbados, St
Lucia and Dominica, re-crossing the Atlantic and arriving at
Las Palmas in the Canary Islands on 30 October. The next port
of call was Gibraltar, and *Hood* returned to Devonport at the
beginning of December.

THE SPECIAL SERVICE SQUADRON

The year 1923 opened with another cruise to Spain and Gibraltar. May saw a change of command, when Mackworth was
succeeded by Captain John Knowles im Thurn and Cowan by
Rear-Admiral Sir Frederick Field, both of whom would prove
to be extremely popular with *Hood*'s ship's company. The first
assignment for the new Admiral was a cruise to Scandinavia,
and the ship visited her old haunts of Stockholm, Kristiania
and Copenhagen in July in company with *Repulse* and the sloop
Snapdragon. She entered the dockyard at Devonport the following month for a refit, during which the searchlights that had
been removed from the tower amidships two years earlier were
restored and her main topgallant mast, which had been
unshipped in March 1920, was refitted.

On 27 November 1923 *Hood* left Devonport for her most important assignment to date—the Cruise of the Special Service
Squadron, or 'World Cruise'. For some months previously
plans had been prepared for a squadron of warships to cir-

TABLE 9: THE CRUISE OF THE SPECIAL SERVICE SQUADRON, 27 NOVEMBER 1923–29 SEPTEMBER 1924

Squadron Commander	Vice-Admiral Sir Frederick Field
Hood	Captain J. K. im Thurn
Repulse	Captain H. W Parker

Commander, 1st Light Cruiser Squadron	Rear-Admiral The Hon. Sir Hubert Brand
Delhi	Captain J. M. Pipon
Dauntless	Captain C. W. Round-Turner
Danae	Captain F. M. Austin
Dragon	Captain B. W. M. Fairbairn
Dunedin	Captain The Hon. A. R. M. Ramsay

Port of call	Arrival date	Distance (nm)
Freetown, Sierra Leone	8 Dec 1923	2,430
Cape Town, South Africa	22 Dec 1923	2,820
Zanzibar	12 Jan 1924	2,300
Trincomalee, Ceylon	26 Jan 1924	2,630
Port Swettenham, Selangor	4 Feb 1924	1,140
Singapore	11 Feb 1924	275
Fremantle, Australia	27 Feb 1924	2,045
Adelaide, Australia	10 Mar 1924	1,260
Melbourne, Australia	17 Mar 1924	460
Hobart, Australia	26 Mar 1924	485
Sydney, Australia	9 Apr 1924	580
Wellington, New Zealand	24 Apr 1924	1,130
Auckland, New Zealand	10 May 1924	550
Suva, Fiji	22 May 1924	1,050
Honolulu, Hawaii	6 Jun 1924	2,720
Vancouver, Canada	25 Jun 1924	2,210
San Francisco, USA	7 Jul 1924	695
Panama Canal	23 Jul 1924	2,990
Kingston, Jamaica	26 Jul 1924	475
Halifax, Canada	5 Aug 1924	1,600
Quebec, Canada	19 Aug 1924	750
St John's, Newfoundland	6 Sep 1924	815
Devonport, England	29 Sep 1924	1,700
Total distance sailed		33,110

The foregoing were the principal ports of call—many other locations were visited during the Cruise—and distances are approximate. The Squadron departed from Devonport on 27 November 1923.

cumnavigate the globe, calling at far-flung outposts of the Empire and Commonwealth in order to strengthen the links between the dominions, colonies and protectorates and the mother country and to demonstrate to the world the power and reach of the Royal Navy. Two battlecruisers, *Hood* and *Repulse*, led the Squadron, and they were accompanied by five of the latest 'D' class 6in-gun light cruisers. The problem of logistics was enormous. The ships—and *Hood* in particular—would be hosting receptions, entertaining VIPs and admitting swarms of visitors month after month for almost a year, and catering and victualling facilities, military parades and guides armed with information for the casual caller all had to be organised. Paintwork had to shine, decks gleam and brightwork dazzle. Not all the activities were designed with public relations in mind, however: the Squadron was composed of warships, and exercises and drills continued throughout the Cruise, honing the vessels and their companies into ever more effective fighting units.

Left, upper: Melbourne, Australia, during the World Cruise, March 1924. There are plenty of visitors to cope with. *John Scott/Peter MacKie Collection*

Left, lower: World Cruise: *Hood* in New Zealand, April/May 1924. The massive main turret rangefinders are much in evidence in this view, as is the pronounced sheer of the hull aft. The after 15in guns appear to be at full 30° elevation. *HMS Hood Association/Johnson Collection*

Below: Another photograph taken in New Zealand during the World Cruise. Tompions bearing the ship's crest were customarily positioned in the muzzles of the 15in guns during peacetime. *HMS Hood Association/Johnson Collection*

The political dimension was expertly handled by Field, promoted to Vice-Admiral at the time of the Cruise. He charmed his visitors, captivated the press, winning over the occasional hostile element within it, and delighted his audiences with his speeches—even in San Francisco, one of the few ports of call in a 'foreign' country. A difficult moment came in Singapore, where Field had to deal with the unease in some quarters concerning the new naval base that was under construction there, and another came in Canada, when he suggested that a couple of cruisers stationed on the west coast would be a valuable asset in time of war and was accused in the press of dictating Canadian naval policy. In general, however, the Admiral carried out his duties as unofficial ambassador with great credit—as, indeed, did the crews of all the ships in the Squadron.

After her return *Hood* was assigned to the Atlantic Fleet, and in October 1924 she entered the dockyard at Rosyth for a minor refit, during which the two searchlights which had been re-installed the previous year were once again removed, the main topgallant mast was unshipped and the two 9ft range-

finders in the control top were exchanged for 12ft rangefinders. The work was completed in December, and in January the ship left for another Mediterranean cruise (in company once more with *Repulse*), visiting Lisbon to represent Great Britain in Portugal's marking of the 400th anniversary of the famous navigator Vasco da Gama, who had discovered the sea route to India in 1497.[3] *Hood* also visited Majorca and Gibraltar, returning home in March. In May 1925 Vice-Admiral Field was replaced by Rear-Admiral Sir Cyril Fuller, and Captain im Thurn by Captain H. O. Reinold. For the remainder of the year the ship was in home waters, and in December she entered the dockyard at Rosyth again, where the original 2m high-angle rangefinder for the 4in anti-aircraft guns was replaced by a 15ft device and the searchlights flanking the rangefinder were repositioned. Much of 1926 was spent in home waters, punctuated by a scare during the General Strike in May that year, when crewmen from the battlecruiser were deployed to guard dock installations on the Clyde.

Fuller flew his flag for the annual Spring Cruise to Gibraltar in early 1927 and the ship paid off in May. She was recommissioned flying the flag of Rear-Admiral Sir Frederic Dreyer, with Wilfred French as Captain. Dreyer's tour of duty lasted until April 1929, during which time *Hood* conducted the usual Autumn and Spring Cruises, carrying out gunnery practice, boat drills, anti-torpedo tactics, replenishments and all the

Right: Port-side detail amidships, 1925, with two of the 5.5in guns and the Admiral's personal transport prominent. *HMS Hood Association/Reinold Collection*

usual chores fundamental to the upkeep and efficiency of the ship.

REFIT

By the late 1920s it was becoming increasingly evident that a modernisation programme for the Royal Navy's capital ships would need to be implemented. The major concerns were the risks associated with air and underwater attack (from both mines and torpedoes); as far back as 1921–22 the Washington Conference had recognised this when the delegates had agreed that existing displacements could be increased by up to 3,000 tons per ship in order to counter these growing threats. *Hood* entered the dockyard at Portsmouth early in June 1929 for a refit that would keep her out of commission for two years. The ravages of almost a decade in service had taken their toll, and major repairs were required to her hull, her main machinery needed to be overhauled and her auxiliary systems required attention. Her underwater protection was considered to be adequate: of more recent vintage than most of the other capital ships in the Navy, *Hood* had incorporated more advanced features than her predecessors.

Her air defences were, however, totally unrealistic, four 4in guns hardly being sufficient to counter a determined onslaught from the increasing number of carrier-based aircraft that now constituted a significant element in the world's leading navies. The new battleships *Nelson* and *Rodney*, recently completed, had shown the way: they were equipped with a secondary battery of 6in guns which could be elevated at 60° and hence used against aerial targets; half a dozen 4.7in long-range anti-aircraft guns, which could also be aimed at surface targets; and eight of the brand new single-barrel 2pdr ('pom-pom') guns, of which much was expected. There was no prospect of fitting *Hood* with such a comprehensive system—for one thing, the funds were not available—but some modifications were carried out to increase her ability to defend herself against close-range air attack. Two eight-barrel 2pdr 'pom-poms' (Mk M, for 'Multiple') were fitted amidships, abreast the funnels, displacing the 32ft cutters that had been rigged there; the shel-

Right: A 4in HA gun crew in action. Four of these weapons were fitted to *Hood* when the ship was completed, and they served aboard until just before the outbreak of World War II. They comprised the ship's only means of anti-aircraft defence until the 1929–31 refit, when they were supplemented by eight-barrelled 2pdr 'pom-poms'. *HMS Hood Association/Willis Collection*

Far right: *Hood's* secondary armament comprised twelve 5.5in guns in single mountings; this is the port mounting on the shelter deck. Each gun required a crew of nine men, could be hand-loaded, and fired at a maximum rate of twelve rounds per minute. *HMS Hood Association/Willis Collection*

Right, lower: Port No 3 5.5in gun drill, circa 1934. At shelter deck level, forward, can be seen an eight-barrelled 2pdr 'pom-pom' mounting, one of a pair installed during the ship's 1929–31 refit. *HMS Hood Association/Willis Collection*

ter deck was locally extended outboard to facilitate the work of the gun crews. Directors were to be installed in protected positions at the after corners of the foretop, but in the event only one was fitted although the position for the other was made ready. A High Angle Control System Mk I was installed at the after end of the after control position; this comprised a 12ft rangefinder with its associated instruments and transmitting equipment, and it replaced the earlier 2m rangefinder. Little could be done with the secondary armament; however, since it elevated to 30° it had some role to play in defending the ship against air attack, and accordingly an experimental control system for barrage fire was fitted to the ship.

The practice of equipping capital ships with their own aircraft had also been kept constantly under review throughout the 1920s. The Zeppelin threat had disappeared with the defeat

Above: *Hood* circa 1928, prior to her first major refit. *John Roberts Collection*

of Germany, but there was a good case for retaining the spotter/reconnaissance type aircraft. The problem was that, ideally, these required three crewmen, pilot, observer and telegraphist/air gunner, which resulted in a much larger aircraft than the two-seat spotter type that had been flown from gun turrets, demanding a higher launch speed and therefore something other than a short take-off platform atop a gun turret; moreover, a retrievable aircraft was of considerably greater value than one which had to be abandoned after its first launch. These questions could be addressed by the shipboard catapult and the floatplane; the latter could land near the mother ship, taxi and be hoisted aboard by means of a handling crane. *Hood* was one of the first ships to be fitted with such equipment, which appeared during the 1929–31 refit. The catapult, which was designated Type F IV H, was activated by means of compressed air. A mock-up was installed on 'X' turret, but for reasons unknown this was not proceeded with and it was finally located on the quarterdeck. Even on a ship of *Hood*'s dimensions it had to be folded when not in use so that it could be stowed fore-and-aft, and during deployment it was rotated outboard into the most favourable wind for take-off. The handling crane was situated abaft the catapult, immediately forward of the ensign staff. The aircraft carried was the Fairey IIIF, the ubiquitous workhorse of the Fleet at that time.

Right: *Hood* fires her after turrets; the photograph dates from about 1926. The somewhat incongruous-looking garden seat was a typical item aboard capital ships of the time. Note the wireless transmitter trunk extending upwards from the shelter deck at the extreme left of the photograph. *HMS Hood Association/Reinold Collection*

Other modifications made during the refit included the modernisation of the wireless transmitting and receiving gear, and the remounting of the 5.5in range-finders in the spotting top in strengthened towers, while some adjustments were also made to the foremast super-structure platforms. On completion of the refit the ship was inclined again, and displacement was shown to have risen by over 1,000 tons and draught increased by a further 6in or so, although much of this could be explained by extra oil bunkerage that had been worked in.

The refit cost £687,000. On 12 May 1931, at its conclusion, *Hood* recommis-

Left: A Fairey Flycatcher sits atop 'B' turret with *Hood* under way, about 1926. Although the turret is trained to starboard, there is no evidence from the photograph that any flying is anticipated. *John Roberts Collection*

sioned as the flagship of the Atlantic Fleet's Battle Cruiser Squadron.

MUTINY

'September 1931 marked the watershed of English history between the wars,' wrote A. J. P. Taylor.[4] On 24 August that year, in response to a budget crisis, a National Government was formed under Ramsay MacDonald, Labour Prime Minister since 1929, in an attempt to deal with the problem. A budget deficit of £170 million was looming, and in order to tackle this a number of measures were proposed by Chancellor of the Exchequer Snowden, among them a cut in pay for all those whose wages (or benefits) were paid by the state. Among those affected were, of course, members of the armed forces. At this time *Hood* was at Invergordon, the Navy's base located on the Cromarty Firth on the east coast of Scotland, in company with other ships of the Atlantic Fleet. Her commander was now Captain J. F. C. Patterson, while Rear-Admiral Wilfred Tomkinson, the ship's former captain, was Rear-Admiral Commanding the Battlecruiser Squadron, flying his flag in *Hood*; in fact Tomkinson was in temporary command of the entire Atlantic Fleet because the Commander-in-Chief, Admiral Sir Michael Hodges, was indisposed.

The press got wind of the proposed pay cuts and on 11 September headlined its findings—some of which were wildly exaggerated—before any official announcements could be made. Unrest spread among the warships and ashore. Disturbances broke out again on 14 September, and there was talk amongst the crews of some of the capital ships that they would prevent the ships from sailing on manoeuvres the following day. Meetings were held and demonstrations took place throughout the 15th and the situation gradually worsened. Tomkinson sent frantic signals to the Admiralty informing them of the deteriorating problem, at the same time instructing

Right, upper: A photograph dated 27 June 1931, with Fairey IIIF S1535/'97' of 444 Flight on the folded quarterdeck catapult. The HACS Mk I on the after control position, also newly fitted, stands out clearly. *John Roberts Collection*
Right, lower: *Hood* with aircraft handling crane deployed, July 1931. Notice that a range clock is still fitted on the after superstructure at this time. *Dick Cronin Collection*

officers to explain the nature of the reductions in pay to the
men and assuring them that their grievances would be listened
to; without condoning the actions of the disgruntled sailors,
he did tend to sympathise with their plight. The threat of force
was open to him, but he never used it.

The 'mutiny' ended when the Board of Admiralty ordered
the ships of the Fleet to return independently to their home
ports with a promise that steps would be taken to adjust the
pay cuts in favour of the lower decks. One by one in the evening

Below: *Hood* under way at a gentle speed, 1931–32. On the port quarter of the foretop can be seen one of the new 'pom-pom' director positions (added during the 1929–31 refit, although only the starboard unit actually had the director installed); forward of this is one of the pair of new 12ft rangefinders for the 5.5in armament (which were removed in 1932 to alleviate the bad vibration experienced in the foretop). *John Roberts Collection*

of 15 September the big ships were unmoored and got under way, whereupon *Hood*'s company reluctantly decided to follow suit. An investigation by the Admiralty resulted in the jailing of some of the instigators of the affair and the discharge from duty of others. To general surprise, Tomkinson was castigated for failing to take the necessary preventative measures in the first place. The pay cuts were limited to 10 per cent all round; on 21 September an emergency Act of Parliament suspended the Gold Standard; the value of the pound Sterling in

relation to foreign currencies fell by 25 per cent; and within a week or so all was as if nothing had changed.

In January 1932 *Hood*, in company with *Repulse*, the heavy cruisers *Norfolk* and sister-ship *Dorsetshire* and the light cruiser *Delhi*, paid a visit to the West Indies, taking in Madeira, Barbados, St Vincent, Grenada and Trinidad, and it was during this cruise that Tomkinson learned that he was to be relieved of his command eight months earlier than scheduled, apparently because of his handling of the 'mutiny'.

In a refit at Portsmouth in the spring of 1932 the aircraft catapult and its associated handling crane were unshipped. The installation had been generally unsuccessful, mainly because at speed or even in moderate seas the ship's quarterdeck was frequently awash and the equipment was unusable—a point made plain during the voyage to the West Indies. *Hood* never carried any aircraft again. The foretop 5.5in rangefinders were also removed during this refit.

THE 'DEPRESSION CRUISE'

In the summer of 1932 Tomkinson was succeeded by Vice-Admiral Sir William James,[5] who brought with him a new Captain, Thomas Binney. To James and Binney fell the difficult task of rebuilding morale throughout the ship after the affair at Invergordon. In fact their remit was wider than that, because one of the first tasks of the two men was to sail the ship along the East Coast, calling at various resorts in order to demonstrate the Navy's prowess and lift morale during the so-called 'Great Depression'. It was a 'World Cruise' again in miniature, with children's parties taking the place of official receptions. Rumours of unrest surfaced from time to time throughout the year, but James' and Binney's firm handling of potential trouble reaped dividends and discord was avoided. Gradually *Hood* became a 'happy ship' once more, helped by encouraging results in gunnery exercises and sporting contests.

Spring 1933 saw the by now routine Spring Cruise to Gibraltar, on this occasion taking in Algiers and Tangier. Back at Portsmouth on 31 March, the ship underwent another refit, lasting but six weeks, during which quadruple 0.5in machine

Right: Full ahead, probably early 1933. The flying-off platform on 'X' turret was removed during the 1929–31 refit and the quarterdeck catapult subsequently installed was unshipped in spring 1932, but, curiously, the platform on 'B' turret, evident here, was not removed until late 1933. *HMS Hood Association/Willis Collection*

guns were fitted at the forward end of the signal platform on the bridge. This was another concession that the danger to capital ships from aircraft was a growing one, although the weapon could only be used at extremely short ranges and its projectile, weighing just over an ounce, was not very impressive. However, it was considerably more potent than the guns the aircraft themselves carried for air-to-air combat, and

much was expected of it. The extensible flying-off platform was removed from the top of 'B' turret at this time.

Binney departed in August that year, to be replaced by Captain F. J. B. Tower. In October, during exercises off the coast of Scotland, the press got wind of a wargame played out by *Hood*'s crew in which landing parties were put ashore to round up other members of the ship's company who were acting out the role of fleeing corsairs. The so-called 'Pirates of Cromarty' incident was totally misinterpreted as a further mutiny, and news of the 'uprising' was circulated around the world. The Admiralty were not amused, and were forced to issue official denials.

The Spring Cruise of 1934 was followed by a short visit to Lagos in West Africa, and on 1 August the ship docked at Portsmouth for another minor refit, during which the 5.5in directors that had been removed two years earlier were re-installed, this time on the Admiral's signal platform abreast the bridge. The 'pom-pom' director positions on the foretop were moved inboard to occupy the old 5.5in director positions, although only the starboard director itself was fitted. While

Below: *Hood* in 1932 or 1933. Courtesy of John Roberts

the ship was under repair James was replaced by Vice-Admiral Sidney Bailey.

COLLISION COURSES

The 1935 Spring Cruise took *Hood* south once again, in company with the battlecruiser *Renown*, destroyers and submarines to the north-west corner of Spain, an old haunt. Exercises were

planned for 23 January off the Ria de Arosa, one stage of which would involve the two big ships sailing on divergent courses to conduct inclination tests and then converging to take up station in line ahead, with *Hood* leading. All went well until the final manoeuvres, when a misjudgement of speed and distance forced *Renown*'s captain to order engines full astern.[6] It was too late. *Renown*'s bows crunched against the flagship's starboard quarter, bounced back and then struck again further aft. *Hood*'s outer propeller was badly damaged and areas of lower plating were stove in and framing buckled.

The matter was serious, and Bailey, Tower and H. R. Sawbridge, *Renown*'s captain, were court-martialled. Bailey and Tower blamed Sawbridge and Sawbridge blamed Tower. But the court found in favour of *Hood*'s Admiral and Captain, and Sawbridge was dismissed from duty. However, the Admiralty,

Right: The collision with HMS *Renown* off the north-west coast of Spain, 23 January 1935.

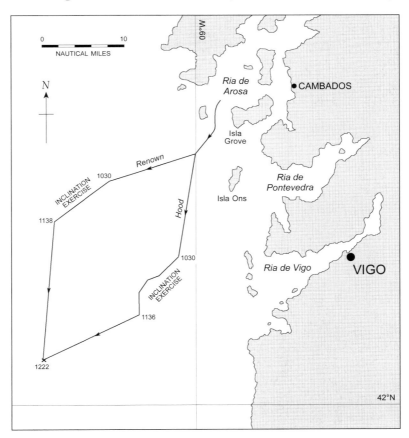

Far left: A view aft from the after control position, about 1934. The single 4in HA mountings are under wraps. *HMS Hood Association/ Willis Collection*
Left: Taking it green, about 1934, the forward 15in turrets trained to port to discourage the ingress of spray. *HMS Hood Association/ Willis Collection*

85

Left: A seaman wistfully examines some of the damage caused to *Hood* following the collision with *Renown. HMS Hood Association/ Willis Collection*

Below: A photograph taken probably in early 1934. The 5.5in rangefinder towers have been removed from the foretop but, apparently, have not yet been installed on the signal platform, which latter does, however, feature new quadruple 0.5in machine gun mountings abreast the conning tower. *John Roberts Collection*

Below: Spit and polish was the order of the day during peacetime, testifying to which in this photograph are the gleaming 15in gun muzzles and the white-painted sheet anchor cable. *HMS Hood Association/Willis Collection*

after some deliberation, demurred, spreading the blame more evenly: it had become apparent that there were some irregularities in the statements made by all three men. It was also discovered that bad feeling had existed between the two parties for some time, and after the verdicts this filtered down to the crews of the two ships. Repairs to *Hood* were carried

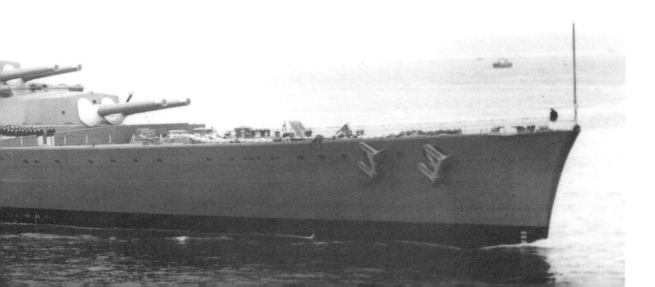

out at Portsmouth and occupied about a week; it was probably during this repair that the missing port 'pom-pom' director was installed at the foretop.

The next major event was the Fleet Review in honour of King George V's Silver Jubilee on 16 July, but by now a political crisis had arisen in the Mediterranean. Mussolini's Italy had been conducting some sabre-rattling against Abyssinia, and in response *Hood*, *Renown* and six destroyers were ordered to Gibraltar in September. But Stanley Baldwin's National Government was reluctant to intervene: the policy of appeasement was well under way and the show of force proved to be a sham. Even when Italian troops invaded Abyssinia in early October nothing was done, and the Government was bought off by Mussolini's promise to send home a division of his troops. *Hood*

Above left: On the Admiral's signal deck, starboard side, mid-1930s. The 24in signalling searchlight is in the foreground, whilst further away from the camera are the two starboard Hotchkiss 3pdr saluting guns. *HMS Hood Association/Willis Collection*

Above right: Hoisting aboard 15in cordite cases adjacent to 'B' turret, mid-1930s. The aircraft carrier ahead of *Hood* is either *Courageous* or *Glorious*. *HMS Hood Association/Willis Collection*

and *Renown* returned to Portsmouth at the end of the month; Tower left his command at the same time, and was replaced by Captain Arthur Pridham.

The ship was at Gibraltar again in early 1936, and was visited by the deposed Emperor of Abyssinia, Haile Selassie, in early May. A 3½-month refit at Portsmouth followed, during which the ship's machinery was overhauled, wireless transmitting equipment was updated, minor modifications were made to the bridge platforms and the spotting-top 'pom-pom' directors were dismantled. These last had been the subject of much criticism owing to their proximity to the forefunnel, smoke from which frequently made sighting impossible, and they were relocated at a lower level, on the rear quarters of the forebridge— hardly ideal positions since in order to function effectively they required clear sky arcs.

THE SPANISH CIVIL WAR

In the meantime international relations continued to deteriorate. The rise of Hitler—and his avowed intention to rearm Germany and redress the 'wrongs' of Versailles—and the adventurism of Mussolini began to dominate British foreign policy. Tentatively, preparations for rearmament were made. 'Collective security'—which meant collective security through disarmament—was still preached, particularly by the Labour Party; great faith was still placed in the

Left: A view from the forepeak, mid-1930s, showing in detail the main capstan (centre) with its attendant rollers and, behind, the three cable holders. Further aft is the forecastle breakwater, almost 6ft high at its centre. *HMS Hood Association/ Willis Collection*
Below: At Malta, probably October 1936. *HMS Hood Association/ Mason Collection*

League of Nations. But the signals were ominous, and the service chiefs, who had for long warned about the dangers from Germany and Italy, and from Japan, were asked to draw up their recommendations. Then, in July 1936, Spanish generals rebelled against the government in Madrid, beginning a three-year conflict that further divided the European nations. Opinion in Britain was ambivalent. An international Non-Intervention Committee was set up, and it became the official policy of the European powers to support neither side. However, Germany and Italy paid only lip-service to the agreement, sending military aid to the Fascists under Franco; Soviet Russia did likewise, supporting the Republican government.

The European navies patrolled the Spanish coast, warily watching each other as they enforced the policy and safeguarded the passage of their merchant shipping—innocent and otherwise. Predictably, there were incidents, in one of which *Hood* was involved. Late on 22 April 1937 three British merchantmen, *Hamsterley*, *MacGregor* and *Stanbrook*, laden with food and other supplies, left the French port of St Jean de Luz en route to Bilbao in northern Spain, some 80nm distant and blockaded by Nationalist warships. *Hood*, now flying the flag

of Vice-Admiral Geoffrey Blake, had been ordered to the area from Gibraltar earlier that month because of rising tension and stood off to the north. As the three British cargo ships approached Bilbao they were challenged by the Nationalist armed trawler *Galerna*, backed up by the 7,500-ton, British-designed light cruiser *Almirante Cervera*, which was armed with 6in guns. The Spanish ordered the merchantmen to heave-to, and the *MacGregor*'s skipper immediately called for assistance to British destroyers in the vicinity. After an exchange of messages the *MacGregor* decided to steam on, whereupon *Galerna* opened fire with a warning shot. One of the destroyers, *Firedrake*, responded by training her guns on the Spanish vessels; in reply, *Almirante Cervera* began to make threatening manoeuvres. At this point Blake decided to intervene, and *Hood* loomed up on the horizon. More shots were heard as coastal batteries opened fire on *Galerna*, which promptly moved off, and Blake trained the battlecruiser's main armament on the Spanish cruiser. The latter took the hint and gave way, and the *Hamsterley*, *MacGregor* and *Stanbrook* docked in Bilbao, unmolested and to a rapturous reception.

Shortly after this incident *Hood* sailed for home to take part in the Coronation Review of the Fleet, where on 20 May she received a visit from King George VI, but by June she was back on patrol off the Spanish coast, this time in the Mediterranean. Blake was taken ill and discharged from duty on medical grounds, and on 15 July his place was taken by Vice-Admiral Andrew Cunningham; he was joined a month later by a new Captain, H. T. C. Walker. Based in Malta with *Repulse* and the aircraft carrier *Glorious*, *Hood* conducted routine patrols in the waters between Barcelona and Valencia, with visits to Gibraltar, Tangier and Palma. Incidents were few.

The ship's anti-aircraft defences were further strengthened in November 1937. Docked at Malta, *Hood* received two additional 4in HA Mk IV guns on the shelter deck, an eight-barrel 2pdr 'pom-pom' mounting at the after end of the shelter deck and another pair of quadruple 0.5in machine guns, one mounting each to port and starboard, adjacent to the after control position. The extra 'pom-pom' mounting was installed on a

Below: Somewhat the worse for wear, *Hood* rides at anchor with booms deployed. The photograph was taken at around the time of the Spanish Civil War, since the blue, white and red neutrality stripes across 'B' turret may be discerned. Note the air defence position now fitted atop the compass platform. *Bibliothek für Zeitgeschichte*

new deckhouse, offset from the centreline to starboard. The advantages of carrying aircraft on board ship were recognised by the mid-1930s, despite the unfortunate experiences of *Hood* during her Atlantic crossing in 1932; indeed, practically all the capital units in the Fleet either had been equipped with a catapult or were scheduled to be so equipped in an imminent refit.[7] Accordingly, it was planned that *Hood* should mount a

new catapult on 'X' turret, well out of
the way of the wetness of the quarterdeck. In order to hoist the seaplane it
would be necessary to install a crane
right aft on the shelter deck, and it was
to make room for this equipment that
the new 2pdr 'pom-pom' mounting was
offset.[8]

Patrols continued throughout the
early months of 1938, and incidents now
abounded. Torpedo attacks on neutral
shipping—both merchantmen and warships—were reported with increasing
frequency, and although nothing could
be proved the Italians were suspected of
being the main culprits. Warnings were
issued and the patrolling warships increased their vigilance.

A short refit at Malta in May and June
1938 saw the removal of the two shelter-
deck 5.5in guns and their replacement by
single 4in HA Mk IV mountings, the installation of a third 'pom-pom' director,
which was sited on the after control position just abaft the HACS director, and
the upgrading of the ship's wireless
equipment. The underwater torpedo
tubes were also removed.

Above: In dry dock at Malta,
probably late 1937. *HMS Hood
Association/Ken Clark Collection*

On 22 August 1938 Cunningham left the ship to take up a
new appointment and Vice-Admiral Geoffrey Layton succeeded him. Then, at the end of September, came the Munich
Crisis. Tension had been building up for some time over Hitler's demands that the grievances of the Sudetens—some three
million Germans living in Czechoslovakia—be addressed; the
fear was that he would impose a 'solution' unilaterally and
bring the entire country under German control, as he had in
the Austrian *Anschluss* six months earlier. In Britain, preparations were made for war: air-raid shelters were dug, plans for

the evacuation of the capital were dusted off, gas masks were issued and on 27 September the Royal Navy was mobilised. *Hood* put to sea from Gibraltar the following day, tracking the German 'pocket battleship' *Deutschland* which was known to have done likewise, presumably in search of prey. Then Prime Minister Chamberlain met Hitler and secured 'peace for our time'. The First Lord of the Admiralty, Duff Cooper, resigned in protest. Appeasement had won the day, and *Hood* returned to Gibraltar. Soccer matches were arranged with the crews of *Deutschland*, which had been permitted to dock there,[9] and life continued much as before.

RECONSTRUCTION?

The Washington Agreement of 1922 had forbidden the construction of new capital ships for the Royal Navy other than *Nelson* and *Rodney*. It was due to expire at the end of 1931, and in anticipation of this a Naval Disarmament Conference was called in London in January the previous year. Agreement was reached by Britain, the United States and Japan, and among its provisions was one extending the moratorium on new battleship building for a further five years. By now, however, the Royal Navy's battle fleet was an ageing asset: other than the two *Nelson*s, its ships were of First World War vintage— indeed, six of them had fought at Jutland. Moreover, trials

Above: In company with the battlecruiser *Repulse* in the Mediterranean. This photograph was taken after December 1937 because the new 2pdr 'pom-pom' mounting fitted on *Hood*'s after shelter deck at Malta at that time is evident. *Bibliothek für Zeitgeschichte*

Right, upper: Patrolling off Spain during the Spanish Civil War. The neutrality stripes around 'B' turret were coloured blue (forward), white and red. *HMS Hood Association/Hayes Collection*

Right, lower: In Malta at the time of the Spanish Civil War. The paint scheme is now a light grey, AP 507C, the standard colour for vessels serving in the Mediterranean at that time. The fore- and mainmasts from a point level with the funnel tops up to the starfish platforms are painted black. *Bibliothek für Zeitgeschichte*

throughout the 1920s had suggested that these vessels were deficient in both horizontal and vertical protection; and, in addition, there was the growing menace of attack from the air, and the ships were ill-equipped to deal with it. The problem was that the Washington Agreement permitted only 3,000 tons to be added to existing individual displacements; furthermore, the additional weight of a comprehensive armour system and a modern anti-aircraft defence

Above: July 1938, at Malta. The two 5.5in guns abreast the forefunnel have been replaced by single 4in HA mountings. *John Roberts Collection*
Right, upper: Spick and span during the final years of peace. Notice the multiple machine-gun mounting and the two saluting guns on the signal deck, and the new air defence position on the roof of the forebridge. *HMS Hood Association/ClarkCollection*
Right: Another photograph taken when *Hood's* shelter-deck 5.5in guns had been supplanted by single 4in HA mountings—which dates the image at between June 1938 and July 1939. However, the presence of the mainmast HF/DF office narrows the date down to June or July 1939. *John Roberts Collection*

would require compensatory reductions in weight elsewhere (for example, in the ships' machinery); and, further again, in the depression-hit years of the late 1920s and early 1930s funds were not available.

Nevertheless, some degree of modernisation was imperative. The five *Queen Elizabeth* class battleships—the core of the Fleet—were accorded priority, and one by one they were taken in hand to have their deck armour strengthened and their AA armament improved. *Barham* was first, in 1931–34, followed by *Malaya* in 1934–36; the *Royal Sovereign* class battleship *Royal Oak*[10] and the battlecruiser *Repulse* received similar refits at about the same time. By the time the third *Queen Elizabeth* class ship, *Warspite*, was due to be taken in hand more funding had become available and it was decided that a complete reconstruction

Below: Another June/July 1939 view, showing some of the ship's inventory of 2pdr, 4in single and 4in twin anti-aircraft guns. *John Roberts Collection*

could be financed; the work began in March 1934 and lasted three years. *Renown* entered the dockyard for similar treatment in September 1936 and the remaining two *Queen Elizabeth*s the following year.

Hood was the most modern capital ship in the Fleet other than the two *Nelson*s, and was accordingly given a much lower priority than all other battleships and battlecruisers apart from the *Royal Sovereign*s, but finally, in December 1938, proposals were put forward for her complete reconstruction. The details of these proposals were never formalised, but it was doubtless envisaged that the ship would be gutted and that, apart from her hull structure and main armament, practically everything would be replaced. Her horizontal protection would be renewed, with 4in or even 5in armour above the machinery and magazines; her turbines and boilers would be replaced by

Above: *Hood* in August 1939, with the shelter-deck 5.5in guns back in position. The HF/DF office on the mainmast starfish, added during the 1939 refit, was removed in 1941. *John Roberts Collection*

modern, space-saving machinery; her bridge and conning tower would be dismantled and replaced with a compact structure in the manner of other recently reconstructed Royal Navy capital ships; eight of the brand new 5.25in dual-purpose guns in twin turrets would replace the existing secondary armament and long-range AA weapons; additional 2pdr 'pom-pom' mountings would be installed; all torpedo tubes would be deleted; an athwartships catapult, probably at forecastle deck level, would be fitted, together with a double hangar for aircraft stowage; and the underwater bulges would be redesigned, their crushing tubes replaced with additional bunkerage. The work was to begin in early 1940, once *Queen Elizabeth* was out of dockyard hands.

In the meantime, much could be done to make the ship more battleworthy—particularly with regard to her air defences—and in the six months from February to August 1939 she was at Portsmouth again for refitting. It was intended to equip her with a complete outfit of twin 4in Mk XIX mountings. These weapons had been introduced to the Fleet some four years earlier and had already been fitted in *Malaya*, *Barham* and some of the ships of the *Royal Sovereign* class. They were intended primarily as an anti-aircraft defence, although since their range of elevation was anything up to 80° they could, like the single 4in guns they were to replace, be employed against surface targets. For reasons that are not entirely clear, these weapons were fitted aboard *Hood* in two distinct stages, the first of which was the 1939 refit. Despite the ship's capacious shelter deck, the edges of the latter had to be extended outboard, over the open batteries of the amidships 5.5in guns, in order to accommodate the new mountings. Two were sited abreast the after funnel and two abreast the mainmast, the latter mountings displacing the singles which had been added there in 1937; some of the ship's boats had to be relocated to make room. The signal platform beneath the bridge was extended well aft, and on each corner of the extensions a Mk III HACS was installed. New high-frequency direction-finding equipment was fitted, its office located on the mainmast starfish, and the searchlight suite was upgraded, with new 44in lights fitted on new deckhouses adjacent to the after control positions and abaft the after funnel. The usual overhauls were given to the ship's machinery, her electrical plant and her auxiliary systems.

The ship was undocked in June 1939, two-thirds the way through her refit, to allow trials of her new 4in twins to be carried out. These were successful, and *Hood* returned to Portsmouth the following month to enable further work to be done. All six remaining single 4in guns were removed, and the 5.5in mountings on the shelter deck abreast the forefunnel, which had been removed at Malta in the spring of 1938, were reintroduced in their original positions.[11] The searchlight tower between the funnels was removed, its place taken by an office for the medium-frequency direction-finding equipment. Finally, the HACS Mk I installed in 1929–31 was replaced by a more up-to-date Mk III model, matching the two new systems installed on the signal platform.

Hood recommissioned on 13 August 1939 when Vice-Admiral William Whitworth raised his flag on her, joining Captain Irvine Glennie, who had been appointed in place of Harold Walker three months beforehand. Tension in Europe was rising to fever pitch. Czechoslovakia had collapsed six months earlier and no one had gone to her aid, but now Hitler was threatening the Poles, to whom the British Government had given a guarantee of support. Rumours of war were rife; and then came the startling news, on 23 August, that Nazi Germany had signed a non-aggression pact with the Soviet Union. Poland looked doomed.

On 1 September 1939 *Hood* sailed to Scapa Flow to await developments.

WAR

T HE DECLARATION of war came on 3 September 1939, at 11 a.m. The ship's company aboard *Hood* heard the news at sea: the ship, together with the battlecruiser *Renown* and other warships of the Home Fleet, was on patrol north of the Shetlands, having left Scapa two days previously in order to search for the German passenger liner *Bremen* and, with luck, to intercept any German raiders that might be attempting a break-out into the Atlantic. It was a fruitless mission—the first of many such sweeps in these waters—and the ships returned to Scapa that day. *Hood* put to sea again on 8 September, this time in company with the light cruisers *Edinburgh* and *Belfast* and escorting destroyers, sweeping the waters between Iceland and the Faröe Islands for any signs of German shipping. She returned on the 12th.

ROUTINE

The first alarm for the ship came on 22 September, during a patrol in the North Sea, when one of *Hood*'s escorting destroyers detected a U-boat. Real excitement was to follow four days later, when, in a sortie reminiscent of Admiral Beatty's exploits during the First World War, *Hood* and *Repulse* were ordered to provide cover for the 2nd Cruiser Squadron, which, with escort provided by the 7th Destroyer Flotilla, was en route to the Horns Reef off Denmark to assist in the salvage of the crippled submarine *Spearfish*, which had been taking part in a concerted effort to blockade German shipping. No German warships interfered, and the submarine was successfully rescued, but on the way home a group of *Luftwaffe* Ju 88 bombers of *I./Kampfgruppe 30*, based on Sylt, attacked the British ships. Taken by surprise, the battlecruisers immediately went to action stations as the German aircraft dived out of the clouds. Within seconds a bomb struck *Hood* on the port quarter, bounced off the hull and exploded in the sea close by, showering the ship with spray and shrapnel. No real damage was done, but the Commander-in-Chief Home Fleet, Admiral Sir Charles Forbes, was not impressed: he had witnessed the attack on board his flagship *Nelson*, and he castigated the crews of the battlecruisers for their laxity in meeting the threat. The Germans made huge propaganda out of the incident, claiming not only that *Hood* had been badly damaged but that the carrier *Ark Royal*, which had also been part of the covering force, had been sunk—the first of many such false claims concerning this ship.

Patrols resumed. On 8 October came the news that the German battlecruiser *Gneisenau*, in company with the light cruiser *Köln* and nine destroyers, had been spotted in the Skagerrak, possibly en route for a break-out into the Atlantic. The Home Fleet reacted, and *Hood* and *Repulse*, plus the two light cruisers *Sheffield* and *Aurora*, were despatched northwards to cover the area off Bergen. Nothing further was reported for two days, when it was announced that the two German warships had turned about and were steaming eastwards. *Hood* returned to Loch Ewe on the west coast of Scotland but quickly put to sea once more to patrol the Denmark Strait in search of German shipping, this time in company with the battleships *Nelson* and *Rodney*, the carrier *Furious* and the cruisers *Belfast* and *Aurora*. It was a routine sortie, and, again, nothing was spotted.

Six weeks had passed since the declaration of war and little of note had occurred, other than the bombing scare of 26 September. As in the First World War, there was little likelihood that the German Fleet would foray in any strength, its

Below: A view of the wardroom aboard *Hood*.

excursions limited to sorties by single ships, or pairs, man-oeuvring close to the European mainland in an effort to draw the Royal Navy within range of land-based bombers. Meanwhile a sort of 'guerrilla campaign' was already well under way. Two German 'pocket-battleships' were on station in the South and North Atlantic by the time war was declared, U-boats were deployed to the North Sea, Bay of Biscay and North Atlantic on 3 September, and minelaying sorties by both U-boats and surface vessels swiftly got under way thereafter. The passenger liner *Athenia* had been torpedoed and sunk as early as the first day of hostilities, and by the middle of the month convoys of merchant ships were being attacked. On 17 September *U 29* sank the fleet aircraft carrier *Courageous* off the coast of Ireland. The danger to the Fleet was emphasised on 14 October when *U 47*, commanded by *Kapitänleutnant* Günther Prien, penetrated the defences at Scapa Flow and fired five

torpedoes at the battleship *Royal Oak*. Two detonated, and the ship sank within a quarter of an hour, taking with her over 800 officers and men. Near-panic ensued, and the Home Fleet was quickly dispersed while the base's defences were hastily re-examined. *Hood* remained at Loch Ewe for the time being. The vulnerability of the warships at Scapa was highlighted again just three days later when a force of Ju 88s, again from I./*KG 30*, raided the base and bombed and crippled the gunnery training ship and ex-battleship *Iron Duke*, which had to be beached as a result.

On 30 October, in company with the battleships *Nelson* and *Rodney*, *Hood* was ordered to sea to cover an important convoy transporting iron ore from Narvik in Norway to Britain. Just north of the Orkneys, a U-boat—*U 56*, under the command of *Leutnant* Zahn—evaded the ten escorting destroyers and fired three torpedoes at *Nelson*. One missed but two struck home, fortunately without effect because they proved to be duds. The ships steamed on, blissfully unaware of the fate that had nearly befallen them, and reached the region of the Lofoten Islands off northern Norway before turning for home.

Hood was sent south to Plymouth in November to await further orders. These came on 23 November, when it was reported that *Scharnhorst* and *Gneisenau* were at large in the Iceland–Faröes passage and were engaging the armed merchant cruiser *Rawalpindi*. All available Royal Navy ships were diverted to hunt for the raiders. *Hood* left port and, with the destroyers *Echo*, *Eclipse* and *Exmouth*, joined up with the French *Force de Raide*, commanded by Vice-Admiral Gensoul and comprising the battlecruiser *Dunkerque*, the 6in-gun light cruisers *Georges Leygues* and *Montcalm* and the 'super-destroyers' *Mogador* and *Volta*.[1] The combined force set course for the North Atlantic for a position south of Iceland; it could not save the *Rawalpindi*, which had gone down to *Scharnhorst*'s guns in a heroic engagement, but the movements of the German warships could not be predicted and a break-out into the Atlantic— and the dire consequences of this for convoy traffic—was a possibility. In the event, the two German battlecruisers had made contact with the cruiser *Newcastle*, and, under orders to avoid action with heavily armed ships and taking advantage of appalling weather, the German admiral managed to slip back home unnoticed.

Hood returned to Plymouth but in early December was sent back to Loch Ewe to prepare for further North Atlantic duty. This time the task was to help cover a very valuable cargo— the first convoy of troops to be sent across the Atlantic from Canada. Designated TC.1, it consisted of the passenger liners *Aquitania, Empress of Britain, Empress of Australia, Duchess of Bedford* and *Monarch of Bermuda* and was escorted by the battleship *Resolution*, the battlecruiser *Repulse* and the carrier *Furious* together with the old light cruiser *Emerald* and the new destroyers *Hunter* and *Hyperion*. This formidable escort was further enhanced by four Canadian destroyers for the first part of the passage and by twelve British destroyers for the last leg. *Hood*, in company with the Jutland veterans *Barham* and *Warspite*, sailed on 13 December to rendezvous about 25°W, to add still more fire power to the escort. The sortie was uneventful, apart from an minor collision involving *Aquitania, Furious* and a steamship voyaging in the opposite direction.

1940 REFIT

The early months of 1940 were passed in much the same way as the previous months, with routine patrols out of Greenock on Clydeside. The ship was able to return to Scapa Flow after the defences there had been overhauled, and on 2 March, accompanied by another Jutland veteran, the battleship *Valiant*, covered a North Sea convoy en route from Norway. On 8 March *Hood* was visited by Winston Churchill, the First Lord of the Admiralty, who had travelled north to inspect the new defences; and on 11 March Vice-Admiral Whitworth left to take up a new command.

The ship was now in need of some attention. Six months of continuous service, most of it at sea, had taken their toll: she could barely make 26 knots, her hull was strained by the huge waves of the North Atlantic winter and leaks were beginning to appear. Her displacement was now the highest it had ever been—48,500 tons at deep load—and waves were not only crashing over the forecastle and quarterdeck but showering her shelter deck too, flooding her anti-aircraft stations and wrecking her boats. Moreover, wartime experience had already demonstrated that shipboard AA defences in general ought to be strengthened.

Hood left Scapa Flow on 27 March and docked at Devonport two days later. During her eight-week stay the entire battery of 5.5in guns was landed, and the embrasures for the two guns either side of the bridge and forefunnel were plated over. Three more twin 4in Mk XIX mountings were added to the shelter deck, one right aft and the other two abreast the after control tower, and splinter plating was fitted to all the AA positions, new and existing. A novel type of AA defence was also introduced to the ship—the Unrifled (or Unrotated) Projector. This was a trainable device comprising twenty launching tubes for firing parachute-retarded bombs into the air in the event of a air attack, the principle being that one or more of the attacking aircraft might become entangled in the parachute cables and detonate the bombs. The UP was typical of the half-baked schemes for air defence that proliferated during the early months of the war, and, predictably, it was singularly unsuccessful. Nevertheless, much faith was placed in it in the spring of 1940, and *Hood* mounted five installations, one on 'B' turret and the other four along the edge of the shelter deck, abreast the forefunnel and between the forwardmost 4in twins. As with the latter, the UPs were given splinter plating, and the missiles themselves were stowed in ready-use lockers adjacent to each mounting.[2] With the original secondary armament now deleted, the 5.5in director towers on the Admiral's signal platform were converted to 4in control towers, for use when the 4in twins were employed in the surface role.

Other work carried out during this refit included the overhaul of the main and auxiliary machinery, repairs to hull plating and the fitting of a degaussing coil around the hull just beneath the deck edges to protect the ship against magnetic mines. The 15ft rangefinder was removed from the foretop, although the director proper and its armoured hood remained

Below: A view of the quarter-deck. This photograph was taken after spring 1940 because what appear to be the barrels of a twin 4in mounting are discernible forward of the after 'pom-pom' on the shelter deck and twin 4in mountings flank the after superstructure. The main turret sighting ports are prominent in this view, which also affords a close look at some of the ventilators situated on the quarterdeck. *Bibliothek für Zeitgeschichte*

Right: Diagram showing the principal features of the Unrifled Projectile (UP). *Author*

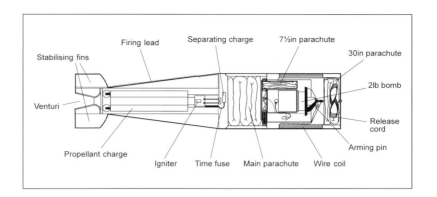

Stabilising fins

Firing lead

Separating charge

7½in parachute

30in parachute

2lb bomb

Venturi

Release cord

Arming pin

Propellant charge

Igniter   Time fuse   Main parachute   Wire coil

in position. The fitting of a catapult on 'X' turret and a handling crane on the shelter deck so that the ship could re-embark a spotter aircraft was seriously considered, but the additional weight was deemed to be too great and the plans were shelved.

While the refit was under way, events in Europe took several turns for the worse with Hitler's seizure of Denmark and his occupation of the major Norwegian ports. The British Government reacted to these events by despatching a force of some 700 men, mostly sailors and Royal Marines, to Åndalsnes and Ålesund, two small ports some 100 and 120 miles, respectively,

Below: The starboard after twin 4in mounting firing at low angle. Notice the rounds stowed alongside the guardrail and the ready-use ammunition locker on the far right of the photograph. *HMS Hood Association/Mason Collection*

south-west of Trondheim. The object of the operation, code-named 'Primrose', was to establish a foothold in Norway. On 13 April some 250 men from *Hood* travelled to Rosyth, where they joined detachments from the battleships *Barham* and *Nelson* and crowded on to four sloops, *Auckland*, *Bittern*, *Black Swan* and *Flamingo*, together with stores and equipment, including anti-aircraft guns. The expedition was hastily planned and a complete failure. The disembarkations in Norway proceeded unopposed, but German aircraft repeatedly bombed the British forces, destroying much of their equipment in the process and practically razing Åndalsnes to the ground. Confused orders followed, and at the end of the month the force, along with other troops who had been landed elsewhere, had to be evacuated.

By the time *Hood*'s refit had been completed, Winston Churchill had become Prime Minister, France had been invaded and Operation 'Dynamo'—the evacuation of the British Expeditionary Force from Dunkirk—was under way. On 27 May the ship steamed north to the Gladstone Dock in Liverpool, where the necessary maintenance on her underwater hull was carried out over the next few days.

En route to Britain at this time was an impressive array of merchant ships, carrying Australian and New Zealand troops for the fight against Hitler. Convoy US.3 made a spectacular sight, comprising as it did some of the largest and finest passenger liners in the world—*Queen Mary*, *Mauritania*, *Empress of Britain*, *Empress of Canada*, *Aquitania* and *Andes*—and, it was felt, it would be a prime target for Axis attack, especially as it entered European waters. Accordingly, every effort was made to ensure its safety. On 14 June, off Gibraltar, escorts were exchanged and it was met by *Hood*, the old carrier *Argus*, the old Royal Navy destroyers *Broke*, *Wanderer* and *Westcott* and the more modern Canadian *Restigouche*, *St Laurent* and *Skeena*, while RAF Coastal Command Sunderlands kept a vigil from the skies. In the event, enemy attacks did not materialise—although a U-boat hunting group was mobilised, it failed to locate the convoy—and the transports arrived at Clydeside on 16 June.

'CATAPULT'

On 18 June 1940, the day after France fell, *Hood* was despatched to Gibraltar in company with the aircraft carrier *Ark Royal* and four destroyers of the 8th Destroyer Flotilla, *Escapade*, *Fearless*, *Faulknor* and *Foxhound*. On arrival these ships teamed up with the battleships *Valiant* and *Resolution*, the 6in-gun cruisers *Enterprise* and *Arethusa*, the destroyers *Escort*, *Foresight* and *Forester* and the eight destroyers of the 13th Destroyer Flotilla, *Active*, *Douglas*, *Keppel*, *Vidette*, *Vortigern*, *Watchman*, *Wishart* and *Wrestler*. It was odd that, with rumours of an impending invasion of the British Isles by Hitler, such a potent force should be assembled in the faraway Mediterranean, but within a fortnight its purpose became clear.

One of the immediate concerns for the British Government following the French capitulation was the fate of the French Navy: it possessed powerful ships, and their acquisition by the Germans could tip the balance of sea power in the Mediterranean, and perhaps elsewhere. The terms of the Armistice between France and Germany made provision for the French Fleet to be disarmed: the ships would not pass into German or Italian control. In fact, the French had secretly decided to scuttle their ships in the event of an attempted take-over by the Germans, but the British were unaware of these plans and had only the terms of the Armistice to consider.[3] Distrusting the German assurances, they decided to act, and French vessels located in British ports and naval bases were, not without incident, swiftly taken over. However, there remained the problem of the Mediterranean Fleet at Mers-el-Kébir, near Oran in Algeria (then a French colony).

On 30 June Vice-Admiral Sir James Somerville raised his flag aboard *Hood* and Force 'H' was officially constituted. His orders were to ensure that all French warships located at Mers-el-Kébir and Oran were transferred to Royal Navy control, either as combatants or under escort to a distant base; or demilitarised so as to be of no value to the Germans or Italians; or scuttled, to the same effect. Failing these options, he was to destroy the ships by gunfire, preferably while they were in port.

Above: Fifteen-inch shells are hoisted aboard ship at Gibraltar, at about the time of Operation 'Catapult'. *HMS Hood Association/ Mason Collection*

On 2 July the Admiralty issued more detailed instructions concerning the disposal of the French Fleet. These laid down four options, which Somerville was requested to put to the French Commander-in-Chief: (a) the French could sail their ships to British ports and 'continue the fight' against Hitler; (b) they could sail with reduced crews to a British port, whereupon the crews would be repatriated if this was their wish; (c) they could sail with reduced crews to a French West Indian port, whereupon the ships would either be demilit-arised or be handed over to United States safekeeping until the cessation of hostilities, the crews being repatriated as before if they so desired; or (d) they could scuttle their ships. Either of the first two options would result in the ships being restored to the French Navy after the war had ended, with compensation being made in the event of their being sunk or damaged; if the second option were chosen, the ships would not be employed in hostilities if so desired, so long as the Germans and Italians adhered to the terms of the Armistice.

In the event of all four options being rejected by the French, demilitarisation *in situ* was acceptable provided that it could be carried out within six hours, and to the satisfaction of the British Commander-in-Chief, and be carried out in such a way that the ships were *hors de combat* for at least a year.[4] If none of the proposals was accepted by the French, the British C-in-C was authorised to sink the ships of the Fleet using 'all means at his disposal'.

In the morning of 2 July Somerville held a meeting with the captains of the larger ships and the COs of the destroyers, plus Admiral Sir Dudley North (Commander-in-Chief North Atlantic), and Vice-Admiral L. V. Wells (Flag, Aircraft Carriers) in order to discuss the situation. The French force at Mers-el-Kébir consisted of the modern battlecruisers *Dunkerque* and *Strasbourg*, the elderly battleships *Provence* and *Bretagne*, the seaplane carrier *Commandante Teste* and the destroyers *Tigre*, *Lynx*, *Kersaint*, *Le Terrible*, *Mogador* and *Volta*; four miles further west along the coast, at Oran, were seven destroyers and four submarines. The harbour at Mers-el-Kébir was protected by mine nets and anti-submarine booms, while on the surrounding hillsides were an array of 6in, 4.7in and 4in gun batteries.

In the afternoon the ships of Force 'H'—less the destroyers *Douglas*, *Escapade*, *Watchman* and *Wishart*, which were on patrol elsewhere—put to sea for Operation 'Catapult'. Later that night a torpedo detonation was spotted from on board the destroyer *Vortigern*, but although the culprit, a suspected Italian submarine, was hunted for over an hour nothing was found. On board the British ships there was grim determination: everybody hoped that a peaceful resolution could be found, but, if not, then perhaps the French could be induced to yield by means of a limited bombardment, minimising the inevitable casualties. The torpedo-bombers on *Ark Royal* would also be employed, to the same end; aircraft from the carrier were already in the air, keeping watch in the skies over Oran for any sign of action by the French.

Captain C. S. Holland, *Ark Royal*'s CO, transferred to *Foxhound* to act as emissary, and in the early morning of 3 July the destroyer was detached to close Mers-el-Kébir. Arriving just after dawn, she signalled the French senior officer, Admiral Gensoul,[5] an invitation to meet Holland to discuss the problem. *Foxhound* was given permission to approach the harbour and she anchored just outside the net defences, and Holland was informed that Gensoul's representative would be willing to meet him. This he did, and he returned to Gensoul with Somerville's written proposals: sail to join up with Force 'H' and continue the war against Germany and Italy; sail with reduced crews to British ports; or sail with reduced crews to the French West Indies, where the ships could be demilitarised.[6] A six-hour deadline was given for Gensoul's reply, at the termination of which his ships would be sunk. An hour later, at 0930, the French ships were seen to be raising steam, and at 1000 Gensoul's reply was received, scribbled in pencil on the British signal form: he reiterated that he would not allow his ships to fall into German hands, and, obviously taking great exception to the British proposals, indicated that he would meet force with force. In the meantime the bulk of Force 'H' appeared over the horizon and settled down for a long wait.

Various messages were passed to and fro, and as a precautionary measure Somerville ordered aircraft from *Ark Royal* to lay mines outside the harbour entrance. The stand-off continued until 1440, when Gensoul signalled that he was willing to negotiate. Holland was despatched once more, and this time he went on board the French flagship, *Dunkerque*, and met Gensoul face to face. The French admiral was irritated, indicating that he would only obey orders from his Government, but it gradually dawned on him that Somerville was not playing games. Meanwhile the Admiralty in London were becoming impatient: they had received no positive news from Somerville and were insistent that 'Catapult' be carried through to its conclusion immediately. Somerville reluctantly complied and at 1715 passed a message to Gensoul that a decision by him to agree to the British ultimatum was required within fifteen minutes, otherwise the Royal Navy would open fire. In response, Gensoul pointed out that his superior,

Admiral Jean Darlan, Commander-in-Chief of the French Navy, had ordered that, in the event of a threatened take-over by German crews, French warships would sail for internment in the United States for the duration of the war or be scuttled. He also indicated that demobilisation was already under way. With no sign of an end to the *impasse*, Holland left *Dunkerque* to return to his ship, noting that she was preparing for action.

At 1755 on 3 July *Hood* opened fire with her main armament for the first time in anger, joining the action even as 15in shells from *Valiant* and *Resolution* were on their way towards the Algerian coast. The range was 17,500yds. The three British capital ships had positioned themselves to the north-west of the harbour at Mers-el-Kébir, ensuring that return fire from the French would be rendered more difficult by their having to range over the Santon headland, that their fire would be

Left: *Hood*'s 'X' and 'Y' turrets in action during Operation 'Catapult', 3 July 1940. The white canvas blast bags of peacetime now have a more sober hue. *HMS Hood Association/Mason Collection*

masked to some extent by the superstructures of adjacent vessels, and that British shells were less likely to land among civilian areas of the base. The French warships were getting under way as the first British salvos arrived; the shells fell short, but those from the second salvos struck the mole at the entrance to the harbour. The French replied in kind, *Dunkerque*, *Strasbourg*, and *Bretagne* opening fire as well as the nearby coastal batteries, which were engaged by the cruiser *Arethusa* in response. The third salvos from the British vessels crashed amongst the French warships; *Bretagne* was struck and exploded in a ball of fire and smoke, and a destroyer also received a direct hit.

Fire continued to be exchanged as the French manoeuvred towards the harbour entrance, Captain Holland being the unfortunate close-range 'spotter' as 15in, 13.4in and 13in shells whined their way over his head. Aircraft from *Ark Royal* buzzed

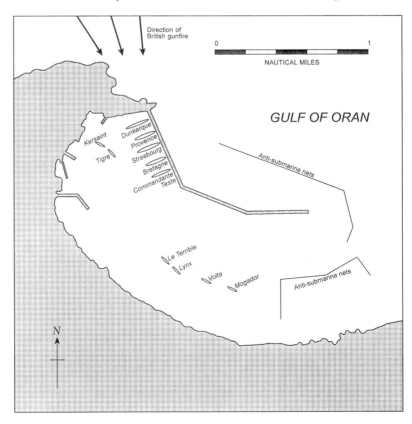

Right: The disposition of the French fleet at Mers-el-Kebir, 3 July 1940. *Author*

over the rising columns of smoke, spotting the fall of shot. The French fire increased in accuracy and *Hood* was straddled,[7] splinters falling on the ship and wounding two men. Gradually, however, the French reply died away, and at 1804 Somerville gave the order to the British ships to cease firing. *Hood* had fired 56 rounds of 15in shell as well as exercising her 4in guns in the engagement. Throughout the 30-minute action Gensoul had repeatedly pleaded with Somerville to cease firing.

When the smoke cleared it could be seen that *Dunkerque* had managed to get under way but had hove-to, badly damaged; *Provence* and *Commandante Teste* were on fire; *Mogador* had stopped also, damaged at the stern; and *Strasbourg* and a number of destroyers were fast making their escape. Somerville waited for confirmation, then Swordfish armed with bombs were launched in an attempt to stop the fleeing battlecruiser. At 1843 *Hood*, the two cruisers and the destroyers worked up speed to give chase, leaving *Resolution* and *Valiant* behind, unscreened, to deal with any other ships that might try to escape. By this time other French warships, from Oran, were approaching the scene, and one, the sloop *Rigault de Genouilly*, was engaged first by *Arethusa* and *Enterprise* and then by *Hood* and *Valiant*—though not before she had fired torpedoes at the British battlecruiser. The missiles passed harmlessly astern.[8]

Strasbourg continued on her way at full speed, and at 1950 six Swordfish torpedo-bombers were flown off *Ark Royal*. They caught the French ship in fading light an hour later and managed to score one hit amidships and possibly another towards the stern, for the loss of three aircraft; these did not slow her, however, and she continued on course. Curiously, Somerville gave up the chase at 2020, citing a long list of hazards—the difficulty of locating the quarry at night; the high speed of the chase, which prevented his destroyers from taking up their proper screening positions; the unfavourable position in which his ships would find themselves were further French naval forces come up to assist; the possibility of losing Royal Navy ships in any engagement; a shortage of fuel. But it must have been apparent that *Strasbourg*'s course was taking her to Toulon, a destination she could not reach for twenty-four hours, and it remains something of a mystery why she was not pursued further.[9]

Force 'H' returned to Mers-el-Kébir, the intention being to launch an air attack at dawn the following day to ensure that *Dunkerque* was disposed of. However, fog prevented an air strike from being launched, and the ships set course for Gibraltar, where they arrived at 1900 on the 4th. That evening and overnight—interrupted by a bombing raid by the French Air Force, which targeted *Hood* but was unsuccessful—the Force was prepared for another assault, this time against the brand new French battleship *Richelieu*. This was a totally different operation, for the ship, not quite completed, was at Dakar in Senegal, 2,000 miles away. However, in an exchange of messages during the night, the Admiralty in London informed Somerville that it was not known whether *Dunkerque* had been totally immobilised (although it was certain that she was aground), and it was decided that he should return to Mers-el-Kébir to administer the *coup de grâce*.

Operation 'Lever', as it was code-named, got under way at 2000 on 5 July with a feint into the Atlantic before Force 'H', less the battleship *Resolution*, turned 180° and made for the Algerian coast once more. At 0250 the following morning Somerville was ordered to call off the bombardment because of possible casualties to the local civilian population and to proceed instead with an air assault. This got under way at 0520 when the first of three waves of Swordfish were flown off *Ark Royal*, and four of the aircraft managed to hit the stranded *Dunkerque*. The second wave was launched twenty-five minutes later and scored two hits, and the third wave rose at 0620 and scored one hit on the battlecruiser and one on the auxiliary *Terre Neuve* alongside. This last proved to be the crucial blow, because the auxiliary erupted in a huge explosion, tearing an enormous gash in *Dunkerque*'s hull. Fire from the coastal batteries, from the foundered battleship *Provence* and from intruding French Air Force aircraft opened up as the third wave lumbered in, and one of the Skuas acting as fighter escort for the Swordfish was damaged. Throughout the operation *Hood* was standing off some 90 miles from the target, ready to intervene if for any reason the air attacks failed. Job completed, however, Force 'H' turned for home, arriving back at Gibraltar at 1830.

The ramifications of Operation 'Catapult' were many and long-lasting. Well over a thousand Frenchmen died in the attacks, and French bitterness towards the British, their allies, lingered for years afterwards. However, distrust of the Germans' intentions was the overriding consideration, and three capital ships that might have been requisitioned by them were rendered unserviceable; the Royal Navy had had to ensure that this was the case, however disagreeable the methods employed.

'HURRY'

Force 'H' formed only one part of the Royal Navy presence in the Mediterranean in 1940; operating from Alexandria in Egypt, at the eastern end of the Sea, was the Mediterranean Fleet under Admiral Cunningham. No sooner had 'Catapult' been successfully completed than the Admiralty in London were firing orders down to Somerville for a new operation which would involve both fleets: divert the attention of the Italian Navy and Air Force from the passage of two important convoys on their way from Malta to Alexandria carrying war *matériel* and evacuees from the island. Force 'H' was charged with penetrating into the Tyrrhenian Sea, close to the Italian mainland. The Mediterranean may not have been Mussolini's *Mare Nostrum* but the Tyrrhenian Sea certainly was, practically encircled by Italian bases on the mainland, in Sicily and on Sardinia. Somerville demurred, suggesting instead an attack on the Italian base at Cagliari in southern Sardinia. He got his way.

On 8 July *Hood*, *Valiant*, *Resolution* and *Ark Royal*, together with the cruisers *Arethusa*, *Enterprise* and *Delhi* (the last a recent recruit to the Force) and ten destroyers, *Faulknor*, *Fearless*, *Foresight*, *Forester*, *Foxhound*, *Douglas*, *Keppel*, *Vortigern*, *Watchman* and *Wishart*, left Gibraltar and steamed east. The ships came under attack from four waves of Italian Savoia-Marchetti SM.79 high-level bombers in the evening of the following day; no bombs found their targets, and one Italian bomber was

Right: Crewmen presumably of a 4in gun mounting—though, if so, well removed from their station—pose before 'A' turret, summer 1940. The wartime censor has done his best to scratch out the UP mounting on 'B' turret but has not entirely succeeded. *John Roberts Collection*

Overleaf: Whilst *Hood* was in the Mediterranean in the summer of 1940 she was on more than one occasion the target for Italian bombers. She survived undamaged, but, as can be seen here, on 9 July she came close to disaster. *John Roberts Collection*

claimed by *Hood*'s anti-aircraft gunners. Although no damage has been done to Force 'H', Somerville weighed the risks: it had already been decided to launch *Ark Royal*'s aircraft for a raid on Cagliari rather than close the base with his big ships and carry out a bombardment, but the carrier had not yet reached her flying-off position and the reception had been very hot. He therefore decided that the danger to his ships was too great, and he ordered a return to Gibraltar. In the meantime, Cunningham's Mediterranean Fleet had met with some success: off Calabria, his ships had tangled with units of the Italian Fleet and the battleship *Warspite* had landed a hit on the Italian battleship *Giulio Cesare* at the prodigious range of 26,000yds,[10] prompting the Italian admiral to lay a smokescreen and scurry off. The Malta–Alexandria convoys got through.

The elderly aircraft carrier *Argus* joined Force 'H' at the end of July, laden with twelve Hurricane land-based fighters bound for Malta. Operation 'Hurry' was devised to ensure that all the aircraft would reach their destination safely, and on the 31st *Hood* left in company with *Valiant*, *Ark Royal* and *Argus*, the three cruisers of Force 'H' and the destroyers *Active*, *Escapade*, *Faulknor*, *Fearless*, *Foresight*, *Forester*, *Foxhound* and *Wrestler*. The

Right: Looking aft from the foretop, 1940. The relative newness of the 4in twin mountings is apparent, and their lighter colour contrasts with that of the rest of the ship. Note the splinter shields fitted outboard of the mountings. *Bibliothek für Zeitgeschichte*

Below: *Hood* at Scapa Flow. The photograph must have been taken in the second half of 1940 because, although the 'B' turret UP mount is prominent, the fore topmast is still shipped, indicating that gunnery radar has not yet been fitted. *John Roberts Collection*

escort also included the destroyers *Encounter*, *Gallant*, *Greyhound* and *Hotspur*, which had arrived in Gibraltar with *Argus*, and these four ships were detached with the carrier after twenty-four hours in order to make their way to Cape Bon on the north-east tip of Tunisia, where the Hurricanes would be flown off. Force 'H' proceeded towards Cagliari in a diversionary sortie, to enable *Ark Royal*'s aircraft to carry out an attack on the Italian airfield and lay mines. *Hood* and her consorts were met by Italian high-level bombers in the evening of 1 August, but again, although there was a near-miss, no direct hits were scored. The carrier attack on Cagliari successful, *Argus*'s mission was accomplished satisfactorily, and the Force turned for home. A full-charge practice shoot of the main armament was conducted en route to Gibraltar, which was reached at midday on the 3rd.

HOME WATERS

The Battle of Britain was by this time at its height and the future was uncertain. The air battle might not be won, and defeat could herald a full-scale invasion of the British Isles by German forces. All naval forces that could be spared were recalled to home waters. For the rest of 3 August and the following morning *Hood* was refuelled and revictualled, and at 1745 she slipped her moorings once more and, together with *Valiant* and *Ark Royal*, steered east into the Mediterranean. It was another feint, for within a few hours she turned 180° and, leaving her companions to continue on their course, she steamed westwards, through the Strait and into the Atlantic. She kept well away from the European mainland, out of reach of inquisitive aircraft, and at 0600 on 10 August she entered Scapa Flow. Meanwhile a new Flag Officer had been appointed: Vice-Admiral Somerville left the ship and in his place Vice-Admiral William Whitworth joined once again.

Hood sailed to Rosyth six days later: the practice shoot of the previous week had revealed some problems with the main gun barrels, and while at Rosyth she had the port barrel of 'A' turret replaced. The ship then returned to Scapa Flow to await developments. One of these came on 13 September, when, in company with *Nelson* and *Rodney*, the old anti-aircraft cruiser *Cairo*, the brand new AA cruisers *Bonaventure* and *Naiad* and eight destroyers, *Hood* was moved to the Firth of Forth, ready to sail south to meet the German invasion fleet should it put to sea. Another came on 28 September, when a German convoy escorted by a cruiser was detected off Norway, but after a foray into the North Sea *Hood* was recalled and returned to Scapa Flow.

Still the ship waited. Then, on 15 October, she sailed once more, this time in company with the 'Tribal' class destroyers

Below: At Scapa Flow in autumn 1940, clearly displaying the degaussing coil fitted around the hull, just below the level of the weather deck. *HMS Hood Association/Mason Collection*

Eskimo, Mashona and *Somali*, to cover the carrier *Furious*—escorted by the cruisers *Norfolk* and *Berwick*—whose aircraft had conducted one of their numerous raids on the Norwegian coast, this time on a seaplane base and oil storage facilities near Tromsø. Bad weather intervened, a thick veil of fog forcing the return of the squadron before it could make its rendezvous. She sailed with *Furious* and a destroyer escort on 28 October to hunt for and intercept German shipping reported to be in the Iceland–Faröes gap, but again the sortie was in vain.

Left: A view from the foremast structure, 1940; the air defence position is at top left in the photograph. The UP mounting (covered) on 'B' turret can be seen. By this time the ship's sheet anchor had been dispensed with. *Bibliothek für Zeitgeschichte*

Yet another fruitless expedition was made early in November, when *Hood* and *Repulse* weighed anchor and sailed in an attempt to intercept the 'pocket-battleship' *Admiral Scheer*. Quite unheralded, the latter had been reported attacking convoy HX.84 off Newfoundland. The auxiliary cruiser *Jervis Bay* had attempted to ward off the German warship with her 6in guns, but she went down after a brief engagement, though not before the convoy had managed to scatter. The German raider, however, caught some of the ships, sinking five and damaging a further three. *Scheer*'s subsequent plans were unknown to the Admiralty, but the Home Fleet was despatched in various directions in an effort to block her routes back to European waters. The two British battlecruisers, accompanied by the anti-aircraft cruisers *Naiad*, *Phoebe* and *Dido* and half a dozen destroyers, steamed into the Eastern Atlantic to cut off any attempted passage to the German-held ports in north-west France. In the event, *Scheer* turned south and was next heard of in the South Atlantic in the middle of December.

Concern with German raiders in the Atlantic was to the forefront during these months, and *Hood* was out again on 23 November, sailing to cover a minelaying operation north of Iceland, the objective of which was to catch enemy ships attempting to break out into the Atlantic or returning from raiding sorties. On 24 December it was the German heavy cruiser *Admiral Hipper* which caused the scare when she was reported as attacking convoy WS.5A and coming under fire from the escorting British heavy cruiser *Berwick*. Once more the problem for the Admiralty was that of covering all possible routes home for the enemy—the Denmark Strait, the Iceland–Faröes gap, the Shetlands–Faröes passage, the Western Approaches. *Hood*, together with the light cruiser *Edinburgh* and the destroyers *Cossack*, *Electra*, *Echo* and *Escapade*, was assigned the Iceland–Faröes passage on this occasion, but yet again no sightings were made: *Hipper*, eluding her pursuers, had set course for Brest in north-west France, and she arrived there safely on 27 December. *Hood* returned to Scapa Flow but sailed again on 2 January 1941 to cover another minelaying operation, this time off the Faröes. Excitement mounted when, on the return, one of her paravanes snared a mine, which was, in the event, safely cut and disposed of by rifle fire.[11]

Hood left Scapa Flow in the evening of 10 January and moored in the Firth of Forth three days later. On leaving Scapa, and in company with *Repulse* and the cruisers *Edinburgh* and *Birmingham*, she had briefly diverted into the Pentland Firth to investigate some mysterious wireless transmissions, but with no result.

On 16 January she was taken into drydock at Rosyth for a refit. The usual standard maintenance and inspection routines were carried out and minor repairs effected, and the boilers and turbines were serviced. Type 284 gunnery radar was installed, its antennas fitted atop and to the forward face of the old director hood at the foretop. To enable the antennas to rotate cleanly, the fore topmast had to be removed; its yardarms were re-fitted directly to the foretop at a lower level, and to compensate for the additional topweight of the equipment the forward portion of the torpedo look-out platform lower down on the foremast was removed. Further aft, the HF/DF station on the mainmast starfish was also removed. New plating was fitted along the old 5.5in battery decks and the complement of ship's boats was updated, the two ancient steam picket boats being replaced by modern 35ft motor-boats. During the refit the ship was visited first by the Prime Minister, Winston Churchill, and then by King George VI. She also embarked a new Captain, Ralph Kerr replacing Irvine Glennie.

The refit was completed on 15 March and within a few days *Hood* was hunting raiders again. Joined by the veteran battle-

Below: Painting ship, autumn 1940. Most of the wartime additions are in place, though radar equipment would be fitted later. The 5.5in guns have all gone, the casemates for the forwardmost pair on either side now plated over. The shelter deck now extends over the entire beam of the ship, supporting the new close-range armament. *John Roberts Collection*

ship *Queen Elizabeth* and the heavy cruiser *London*, both ships fresh from a thoroughgoing modernisation, she swept out into the Atlantic to engage *Scharnhorst* and *Gneisenau*, at large and sinking merchantment. Once again, all possible exit routes had to be blocked. Contact was briefly made by a Swordfish from *Ark Royal*, up from Force 'H' at Gibraltar, and for a while it seemed as though the two elusive German battlecruisers might at last be brought to bay. But it was not to be: by dint of some clever changes of course, Admiral Lütjens, commanding the German force, brought his ships safely to Brest. *Hood* returned to Scapa Flow, disappointed once again.

Post-refit full-power speed trials were conducted in the seas north of Scapa Flow on 25 March, during which the ship made a maximum 28.8kts. This was some 3kts below her best speed, made during the trials run immediately after her completion: the years had taken their toll, her machinery was becoming worn and her displacement had suffered from the numerous alterations and additions made throughout her life. A full-scale reconstruction was needed, as had been carried out to the battleships *Warspite*, *Queen Elizabeth* and *Valiant* and the battlecruiser *Renown* and as had been advocated at the end of 1938 and endorsed by the First Sea Lord the following year. But, for the moment, she could not be spared.

Hood put to sea again on 28 March, patrolling the Bay of Biscay in order to be on hand should *Scharnhorst* and *Gneisenau* leave Brest on another commerce-raiding sortie. British submarines were also sent there in some numbers for the same purpose. *Hood* remained on station for a fortnight, returning to Scapa Flow to refuel on 14 April. Four days later she departed once more, setting course for the same area, and with the same objective. However, she was immediately diverted to the north, news having been received that the new German battleship *Bismarck*, accompanied by two light cruisers and three destroyers, had left Kiel, possibly for a break-out into the Atlantic. In order to cover both the Denmark Strait and the Iceland–Faröes gap, she sailed to Hvalfjord, an inlet north of Reykjavik in Iceland, in company with the light cruiser *Kenya* and a number of destroyers, where, on 28 April, she was

joined by the heavy cruisers *Norfolk* and *Suffolk*. The force made
a foray into the Atlantic to cover some convoys, but the days
were otherwise taken up by routine patrols. Nothing trans-
pired until 4 May, when *Bismarck* was discovered, not on her
way into the Atlantic but in harbour at Gotenhafen in German-
held Poland. With this new threat for the moment out of
harm's way, *Hood* returned to Scapa Flow once again, arriving
there the following day.

On 8 May Vice-Admiral Whitworth said goodbye to the
ship in which he had served, in two commands, for sixteen
months, and on the 12th he was succeeded by Vice-Admiral
Lancelot Holland as Commander of the Battle Cruiser Squadron, Home Fleet. *Hood* remained at Scapa Flow for the next
ten days, venturing out only into the Pentland Firth to conduct
inclination trials in company with the battleship *King George V*
on the 13th and gunnery trials a few days later.

At 2000 on 21 May Admiral Sir John Tovey, Commander-
in-Chief of the Home Fleet, ordered *Hood* to raise steam
preparatory to departing for Hvalfjord once more. It seemed
to be another routine patrol when, at a minute past midnight,
the great battlecruiser slipped her mooring cables and steamed
slowly through the Sound of Hoxa, through the Hoxa Gate,
out into the Firth—and to her appointment with destiny.

Below: *Hood* at Scapa Flow: an atmospheric photograph taken, it appears, at the same time as that on pages 126–127. *Author's Collection*

DEATH

THE TREATY of Versailles of 1919 had placed severe restrictions on the size and composition of the German Navy. The *Reischsmarine* could retain eight antiquated pre-dreadnought battleships, eight cruisers, sixteen destroyers and sixteen torpedo-boats but was not permitted submarines. However, even a fleet of this size would be difficult to operate, because Navy personnel were not to exceed 15,000 in number. New construction was severely curtailed: capital ships of any size were out of the question, since individual displacements were limited to 10,000 tons.

Germany was not a signatory to the 1922 Washington Agreement, nor to the agreement reached at the London Naval Conference of 1930 which reinforced its terms. She was, however, still bound by the conditions of Versailles when she decided to lay the keels for two new *Panzerschiffe* ('armoured ships'), displacing 10,000 tons and armed with 11in guns. Four were originally planned, but only three were completed, and they went on to achieve a good measure of notoriety during the Second World War as the 'pocket-battleships'. The fourth ship was cancelled in favour of a pair of larger vessels, which eventually emerged as *Scharnhorst* and *Gneisenau*, laid down in response to France's new *Dunkerque*s.

In March 1935 Hitler repudiated the terms of Versailles, pointing the way to a German rearmament programme un-

trammelled by treaty restrictions, and three months later this renunciation was implicitly recognised when the British Government concluded a 'private' agreement with Germany over the future size of her Navy. Accordingly, the newly constituted *Kriegsmarine*[1] was authorised to increase its surface fleet to 35 per cent of the total displacement of the Royal Navy and 45 per cent in terms of submarines; capital ships were limited to three in number and to 35,000 tons each in terms of their displacement. The Anglo-German Naval Agreement thus gave Hitler tacit permission—if such were needed—to proceed with major projects. Among these were two new battleships, tentatively identified as 'F' and 'G', design studies for which had begun as early as 1932.

Battleship 'F', otherwise known as *Ersatz Hannover*,[2] was laid down on 1 July 1936 at the Blohm & Voss yard in Hamburg. Her original designed displacement was 35,000 tons and she

Above: The battleship *Bismarck*, photographed in September 1940 and lacking her fire control equipment. *Gerhard Koop Collection*

mounted eight 38cm (15in) guns. A larger calibre, 40.6cm (16in), was considered but rejected because of the delivery schedule involved: design work on a new 38cm gun had begun in 1934, with a view to installing it in *Scharnhorst* and *Gneisenau* at a later date, and in fact by the time Battleship 'F' was laid down the first twin 38cm turrets were in production.

The ship was launched on 14 February 1939, when her name was ceremonially revealed—*Bismarck*. Fitting-out proceeded with alacrity, and the ship was commissioned ahead of schedule on 24 August 1940. She was a handsome vessel, with a graceful clipper bow and a pronounced flare forward, her forecastle deck carried right aft in one long, gentle sweep and her rakish funnel emphasising the classical triangularity of her superstructure. She had eight 38cm guns arranged in the now-standard disposition, two twin turrets forward and two aft, and she boasted a secondary armament of twelve 15cm (5.9in) guns; her anti-aircraft outfit was formidable, with sixteen 10.5cm (4.1in) long-range barrels and sixteen 37mm and twelve 20mm for short-range defence. She could accommodate six aircraft, housed in hangars either side of the funnel and beneath the mainmast and launched by means of a cross-deck catapult amidships. Her armour was strong, with a maximum thickness of 320mm (12½in) along the belt, up to 360mm (14in) for her main armament and a total of 170mm (over 6½in) in two armoured decks. Her splinter bulkheads were placed well inboard of her main vertical armour, requiring the ship to be very broad in the beam but giving her good stability and ensuring that she was very steady in a seaway. When completed she displaced not 35,000 tons but 41,700, thanks to a combination of design miscalculations, requests for design changes and a *laissez-faire* attitude whilst the ship was under construction. In deep condition she displaced well over 50,000 tons, making her marginally the largest warship in the world in late 1940.[3]

THE DANGER

Britain is a trading nation, as much from necessity as from choice; even today she is self-sufficient in relatively few commodities. Historically, one of the roles of the Royal Navy—perhaps the most important role—has been the protection of the shipping lanes along which this trade has been conducted, ensuring the safety of the vessels, of both British and foreign origin, carrying goods to and from the heart of the Empire. The disasters of the First World War, when at one point, in April 1917, a quarter of the merchant ships leaving British ports were sunk by U-boats, were swiftly countered by the Prime Minister, Lloyd George, when he imposed on a reluctant Admiralty the system of convoy, wherein groups of merchantmen sailed together, in formation, under the protection of anti-submarine escorts. Such was the success of the strategy that, on the outbreak of the Second World War, convoys were instituted immediately.[4]

However, there was a crucial difference in 1939: the U-boats were joined by powerful surface raiders in the shape of the 'pocket-battleships' and two large battlecruisers. In the First World War, Germany's capital ships been contained inside European waters by a combination of the Grand Fleet's blockade, the timidity of the German Fleet commanders, a lack of overseas bases and the poor habitability of the vessels themselves; in the Second World War her heavy units had the benefit of a powerful driving force in the form of *Grossadmiral* Erich

Below: *Hood* in 1941, with radar equipment fitted. *John Roberts Collection*

Raeder, the Commander-in-Chief of the *Kriegsmarine*, who ensured that supply ships and tankers were positioned at strategic points in the oceans. Moreover, from the spring of 1940, bases were available to the Germans in both Norway and France, compounding the difficulties of the Royal Navy, which had to concern itself with not one possible escape route—the North Sea—but several.

The havoc which these large surface raiders could cause to merchant shipping carrying foodstuffs, raw materials and war supplies crucial to Britain's prosecution of the war was quickly demonstrated when, on 30 September 1939, the 'pocket-battleships' *Admiral Graf Spee* and *Deutschland* both scored their first successes. The threat to the North Atlantic convoys was more apparent than real for many months of the war, but it was suddenly brought home twice in dramatic style in February/March 1941 when the heavy cruiser *Admiral Hipper* sank or severely damaged ten ships from an unescorted convoy and, in Operation 'Berlin', the battlecruisers *Scharnhorst* and

Gneisenau between them disposed of over twenty vessels in the space of as many days.

It was with considerable apprehension, then, that the Admiralty in London greeted the news on Tuesday 20 May that *Bismarck* had left Gotenhafen in company with a heavy cruiser and was steaming slowly through the Kattegat towards the North Sea. The report had come from the Swedish cruiser *Gotland*, stationed off Göteborg (Gothenburg), and the British Naval Attaché in Stockholm had got wind of it and passed it on to London. The message referred to 'two large warships'; they were unidentified for the moment, but could only be 'pocket-battleships', heavy cruisers or the new battleships *Bismarck* or *Tirpitz*, all of which posed a serious threat if they moved out into the Atlantic.

Below: The heavy cruiser *Prinz Eugen*, which accompanied *Bismarck* in Operation 'Rheinübung' and took part in *Hood*'s final action. She is seen here in May 1941. *Gerhard Koop Collection*

Reconnaissance was vital, and the following day high-flying Spitfires were sent out to photograph the Norwegian coastline in an effort to locate the warships. The afternoon sortie proved fruitful, for tucked up in Grimstadtfjord near Bergen was the unmistakable shape of *Bismarck*, together with that of a *Hipper* class cruiser. The threat had been positively identified; the question now concerned the future movements of the two ships.

'RHEINÜBUNG'

The German *Seekriegsleitung* (Navy War Directorate), flushed with the success of Operation 'Berlin', was anxious to impress upon the German leadership the importance of the *Kriegsmarine*, and particularly the capabilities of its surface fleet and

the role it could play in winning the war: until recent months it had achieved very little apart from the successful campaigns in distant waters of the 'pocket-battleships'. The North Atlantic convoys were the critical target; and, with the growing involvement of the United States Navy, which although nominally neutral was encroaching ever further into the Atlantic providing escorts for eastbound traffic, the task of intercepting them successfully was becoming more difficult as the months passed. Plans were therefore drawn up for a new operation, 'Rheinübung' (Rhine Exercise). *Vizeadmiral* Günther Lütjens, who had led the 'Berlin' sortie, was appointed to command the expedition, which would see *Bismarck* and the *Hipper* class cruiser *Prinz Eugen* break out into the Atlantic Ocean via the northern route and *Scharnhorst* and *Gneisenau* sail from Brest, all four ships meeting up in the Central Atlantic to create a formidable hunting

Left: Another of the few photographs of *Hood* taken after her 1941 refit and therefore showing her final appearance. This uncensored photograph clearly shows the antennas for the Type 284 gunnery radar on the foretop, and three of the UP mountings installed the previous year, one each side abreast and abaft the bridge and one in a 'bandstand' on top of 'B' turret (all are covered to protect the mountings from the elements). Notice the ship's generally dingy appearance, the scrubbed wooden decks of peacetime having been defeated by wear, tear and grime. *John Roberts Collection*

group. The operation had to be modified after an RAF raid on Brest in April 1941 deposited four bombs on *Gneisenau* and again a fortnight later when it was discovered that problems with *Scharnhorst*'s machinery following the 'Berlin' adventure could not quickly be rectified. Now only two ships, not four, would be at large amongst the convoys. A further delay ensued when *Prinz Eugen* was shaken by the detonation of a magnetic mine off Kiel at the end of April, requiring the ship to be taken in for inspection.

Lütjens recast his plans, his doubts about the viability of the operation assuaged by Raeder, who was determined that a show of force amongst the North Atlantic shipping lanes must go ahead; 'Berlin' had proved what could be done. The Fleet Commander decided to make for the Arctic Circle and, once there, determine the best route for a breakthrough into the Atlantic; he favoured the Denmark Strait, as far as possible from the Royal Navy's home bases, out of range of concerted air reconnaissance and where, close to the Arctic icefields, swirling mists might shield his ships from inquisitive eyes. There remained the problem of finding prey. The German Navy had little knowledge of British convoy sailings on the west–east routes: because of the great ranges involved air reconnaissance was out of the question and much reliance was placed on chance encounters, but ocean-going U-boats provided a useful source of information, as did pre-positioned supply ships and tankers. Accordingly, the U-Boat Command was alerted, and a number of weather ships were despatched into the Arctic and Atlantic. The tankers *Esso Hamburg*, *Lothringen*, *Belchen* and *Friedrich Breme* sailed to take up station in the Atlantic and *Heide* and *Weissenburg* set course for the Arctic, while the supply ship *Spichern* sailed from Brest to take up a position in the Central Atlantic.

The preservation of his ships at almost any cost—even that of returning empty-handed—was one of Lütjens' primary considerations. These were his orders. The problem was that, increasingly, convoys were being accompanied not merely by anti-submarine escorts but by cruisers and even battleships. He had confidence that he would be able to deal with any engagement that might eventuate, but the same could not be said of his consort. Accordingly, *Bismarck* was to be employed in, as it were, a reconnaissance role, verifying the status of any convoy that might be sighted before committing *Prinz Eugen* to action; if the odds were even or worse, the two ships were to disengage immediately.

The two German warships slipped their moorings in Grimstadtfjord at 2000 on 21 May and, leaving behind their destroyer escort, *Friedrich Eckholdt* and *Z23*, headed north towards the Arctic Circle.[5] Still there was no definite intent: much would depend on the weather reports, the activities of enemy air reconnaissance and any news of a British reaction. Night was falling: with any luck it would be well into the next day before the absence of the two big ships from the fjord would be noticed.

THE HOME FLEET RESPONDS

Admiral Sir John Tovey, the Commander-in-Chief Home Fleet, was in a dilemma. He had been aware of *Bismarck*'s operational status for some time, and of course there had been the scare of 18 April, when a report that the battleship was putting to sea had proved to be a false alarm. Then came the report of 20 May, and then the confirmation that *Bismarck* had put into Grimstadtfjord. Tovey had to cover all eventualities—or, at least, as many of them as he could with the resources available. The 8in-gun heavy cruiser *Norfolk* was already in the Denmark Strait, on patrol, and her sister-ship *Suffolk* was nearby, refuelling in Hvalfjord. The 6in-gun cruisers *Manchester* and *Birmingham* were close to the Iceland–Faröes gap, where they were ordered to remain pending developments. The battle-cruiser *Hood*, in company with the new battleship *Prince of Wales* and six destroyers, was ordered to sail to Hvalfjord so as to be on hand if the German commander chose either of these two passages.

The most likely exit routes were therefore guarded. Meanwhile RAF Coastal Command was alerted with a view to making a bombing attack on the 21st, and at RNAS Hatston in the Orkneys the Albacore torpedo-bombers of 828 Naval

TABLE 10: PRINCIPAL PARTICULARS OF *HOOD*, 1941

Displacement		42,462 tons light; 48,360 tons deep
Dimensions	Length	810ft 5in pp; 850ft 7in wl; 860ft 7in oa
	Beam	104ft 2in max; 105ft 2in extreme
	Draught	34ft mean deep
	GM	2.99ft light; 3.25ft deep
Machinery	Boilers	24 Yarrow small-tube
	Turbines	Brown Curtis single-reduction geared
	Shafts	Four
	Shaft horsepower	144,000
	Max speed	28.5kts approx
	Endurance	8,500nm at 14kts
Bunkerage	Oil	4,615 tons normal
	Main	Eight 15in 42cal Mk I on twin mountings Mk II; max stowage 120 rounds/gun
	Dual-purpose	Fourteen 4in 45cal Mk XVI on twin mountings HA/LA Mk XIX; max stowage 250 rounds/gun
	Anti-aircraft	Twenty-four 2pdr Mk VIII on eight-barrel mountings Mk VI max stowage 720 rounds/gun; sixteen Vickers 0.5in machine guns on quadruple mountings, max stowage 2,500 rounds/gun; one hundred UP on twenty-barrel mountings
	Saluting	Four 3pdr Hotchkiss on single mountings Mk I; max stowage 64 rounds/gun
	Torpedo tubes	Four 21in above-water
Radar	Gunnery	Type 284
Armour	Belt	12in–7in–5in amidships; 6in–5in forward; 6in aft
	Bulkheads	5in–4in
	Barbettes	12in–3in
	Turrets	15in front; 12in–11in sides; 11in rear; 5in roof
	Conning tower	11in–3in; 6in–3in–2in director hood; 3in tube
	Torpedo conning tower	3in–1½in; 4in–3in director hood; ¾in tube
Protective plating	Forecastle deck	1½in over magazines, 2in–1¼in amidships
	Upper deck	2in over magazines; 1in–¾in amidships and aft
	Main deck	3in over magazines; 2in–1½in amidships; 1in forward; 2in aft; 2in slope
	Lower deck	1in forward; 1½in over torpedo rooms; 2in over magazines; 1½in–1in aft; 3in over steering gear
Complement		1,418

Air Squadron were readied for a possible strike on the two big ships should they sail and flew north to RAF Sumburgh at the southernmost tip of the Shetland Islands in order to reduce the range.

The bombers moved in on the Norwegian coast late in the evening of 21 May but, to their chagrin, the crews were totally unsuccessful: none could find their target. No better fortune favoured the raid the following morning, when low cloud shielded the target area and the bombers were forced to un-load and hope for the best. The bombs fell harmlessly in the fjords and on the surrounding hillsides. As to whether the Ger-man ships were still in Grimstadtfjord, Tovey was none the wiser. Then, at 1630, a Martin Maryland target-towing aircraft of 771 NAS, crewed by Lieutenant N. E. Goddard and Com-mander G. A. Rotherham, took off in foul weather from RNAS Hatston, overflew the target area and, through a cloud break, discovered that the German warships had gone.

Tovey received this news at 1939 with mixed emotions. Had *Bismarck* and the *Hipper* class cruiser been present, then there was still a chance of a successful bombing or torpedo attack in the hours that followed, but now that they had left their anchorages they would have to be positively located before such could take place. Their destination was unknown: they could be en route for a break-out into the Atlantic; they could be on their way to the Arctic as a feint; or they could have turned back for the Baltic. However, he at least now had some definite information and could make further dispositions—and he had to prepare for the worst.

He had immediately available his own flagship, *King George V*, sister-ship of *Prince of Wales*; the brand new aircraft carrier *Victorious*, which had been in commission for a few days only and had as yet no permanent aircraft complement; the cruis-ers *Arethusa*, *Aurora* and *Galatea*, sister-ships armed with 6in guns; *Kenya*, a new 6in-gun cruiser; *Hermione*, one of a new class of anti-aircraft cruisers armed with 5.25in guns; and the des-troyers *Active*, *Inglefield*, *Intepid*, *Lance*, *Nestor* and *Punjabi*. In ad-dition, the battlecruiser *Repulse* was on hand, diverted from the Clyde where she had been making preparations to escort a westbound North Atlantic convoy. Finally, there were the Sunderland and Catalina flying boats of RAF Coastal Com-mand, which were directed to overfly all possible break-out routes in an attempt to locate the German warships. *Arethusa* was sent to join *Manchester* and *Birmingham* to patrol the Ice-land–Faröes gap, but the remaining ships were ordered to raise steam to accompany *King George V*, and late in the evening of 22 May the Home Fleet got under way.

Below: The battleship *Prince of Wales*. A powerful and up-to-date unit, she was however sent into action against *Bismarck* and *Prinz Eugen* without having worked up and she suffered accordingly. *John Roberts Collection*

INTO THE DENMARK STRAIT

Twenty-four hours out from Scapa Flow, *Hood* and *Prince of Wales*, accompanied by the destroyers *Achates*, *Antelope*, *Anthony*, *Echo*, *Electra* and *Icarus*, were ploughing their way through the North Atlantic swell. *Prince of Wales* was a new ship, ordered as one of a class of five battleships on the expiration of the London Naval Agreement and in response to new building programmes being undertaken by Germany and Italy. A second London Naval Conference in 1935–36 had resulted in agreement between Great Britain, France and the United States to limit the maximum calibre of battleship guns to 14in, while the 35,000-ton displacement limit was to remain in force, and the five ships of the *King George V* class were designed within these constraints.

The new battleships were originally to have mounted twelve 14in guns, but because of excess weight 'B' turret was reduced in size to mount twin barrels only; in the event, however, the designed displacement was exceeded, and *Prince of Wales* was commissioned on 31 March 1941 at something nearer 36,700 tons. She was well armoured, her machinery developed

110,000shp and gave her a speed of 28kts, and she was outfitted with the latest search and gunnery radar. However, she had been completed in a great hurry, and evaluating the main armament had been plagued with difficulties; indeed, she had not had time to exercise it in full-scale gunnery trials, and workmen from her armament contractors, Vickers-Armstrong, were still on board trying to sort out all manner of niggling problems when she left Scapa Flow. Her sister-ship *King George V* had been completed at the end of 1940 and had demonstrated that the complexity of her main armament loading arrangements could result in jamming. Nevertheless, these faults had been cured on this particular ship, and there was optimism that the necessary 'fine-tuning' to *Prince of Wales*'s guns could be completed rapidly.

Thursday 22 May had passed without incident, although the news from the Admiralty that *Bismarck* and her accompanying cruiser had left Norwegian waters meant that, instead of entering Hvalfjord, the Battle Cruiser Squadron (as it was somewhat incongruously termed) would remain at sea south of Iceland, ready to intercept the German warships should they pass through either the Denmark Strait or the Iceland–Faröes gap. *Hood* was leading, with *Prince of Wales* off the starboard quarter at the standard distance of four cables.[6] The mood of the crews had been relaxed: this was, after all, still just another routine sweep.

The day had also seen the heavy cruiser *Suffolk* scurrying northwards from her refuelling base at Hvalfjord to join Rear-Admiral W. F. Wake-Walker, aboard *Norfolk*, on patrol in the Denmark Strait. She made contact with her sister-ship at 1000 the following morning. Both ships were well endowed for the scouting role, being fitted with radar equipment; and *Suffolk* had the newest Type 284 gunnery radar, which, although restricted in its arcs, could also function as a surface warning set. Following the rendezvous, *Suffolk* was deployed to the more northerly patrol line, running north-east/south-west close to the edge of the Greenland pack-ice, and *Norfolk* was routed further south, closer to the Icelandic coast. The navigable channel to be kept under surveillance varied in width

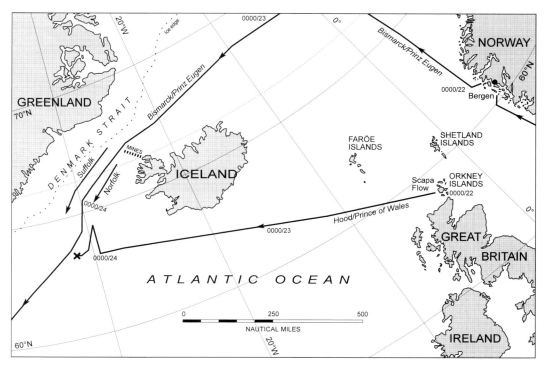

Above: The Denmark Strait—the approach. *Author*

between 100 and 250 miles, but it narrowed considerably off the north-west coast of Iceland because of the British mine-fields which had been laid there: if *Bismarck* and her consort chose the pass through the Strait, there was a good chance that they would be found.

Friday 23 May was another day of routine for *Hood* and *Prince of Wales*. As the waves picked up and the wind strengthened, Admiral Holland outlined his strategy to the senior officers aboard both ships regarding the encounter that might or might not come to pass. The guns were turned and checked, and *Prince of Wales*'s Walrus aircraft was given a final inspection, ready to carry out reconnaissance duties if the weather improved. The destroyers *Anthony* and *Antelope* were detached at 1400, under orders to proceed to Hvalfjord to refuel. Then, at 2002 in the evening, came an intercepted report from *Suffolk*: a battleship and a cruiser had been spotted bearing 020°, course 240°, range seven miles. That placed the enemy virtually due north of the Battle Cruiser Squadron, at a distance of about 300 miles.

In the Denmark Strait Able Seaman Alfred Newell, scanning the misty waters from his look-out position on the starboard side of the cruiser, had spotted first one, then two ships bearing Green 140, that is, off the starboard quarter. He had made his report at 1922 and *Suffolk* thereupon veered away to port, anxious to avoid being seen. When out of visual range, she dropped her speed and allowed the two German ships to overhaul her, finally taking up station on the enemy's port quarter. The two ships had been quickly identified, and the information was relayed to Wake-Walker aboard *Norfolk*, who immediately took up a shadowing position to starboard and astern of the enemy's estimated location. He ventured a little too close, in fact, for at 2030 the two German warships suddenly appeared out of the fog, bearing down upon him at a range of about 10,000yds. *Norfolk* put her helm hard over to starboard, but she had been noticed. Three salvos of 38cm shells crashed around the ship in rapid succession, sending up vast pillars of water and drenching the cruiser with spray and splinters. Sending an urgent report of her plight, *Norfolk* managed to extricate herself from her perilous position and safely regain the cover of the Arctic mists.[7]

THE STRATEGY

Upon receiving *Norfolk*'s report, Holland ordered successive increases in speed for the Battle Cruiser Squadron, first at 2045 to 26kts and then at 2054 to 27kts. Concerned that his escorting destroyers would be unable to match the speed of the big ships, at 2105 he signalled to them to follow as best they could. In the meantime he continued to plot his strategy.

First, unless the enemy, figuratively speaking, changed tack, he, the enemy, was on a converging course with *Hood* and *Prince of Wales*; the opposing forces were some 300 miles apart at 2000, the enemy was steering 240° and Holland himself at 295°, and simple geometry told him that, if he was due south, and given constant speeds, he could expect to intercept after about 320 miles' steaming, or in about eleven or twelve hours' time, that is, at about 0700 or 0800 the following morning.[8] Secondly, it was vital that contact with the enemy be maintained by the two heavy cruisers: everything depended upon it, for, once lost, the enemy might not be found again before he had got among the merchant traffic in the North Atlantic. Moreover, at 2000 he had no knowledge of the enemy's speed; such information could only be pieced together in the light of frequent reports from the two shadowing warships. Thirdly, he had to maintain the element of surprise, and for this reason he forbade the use of either ship's radar equipment, lest the transmissions be picked up by the enemy.[9] Fourthly, there were the details of the interception itself. He did not wish to become entangled in a stern chase, which would restrict his gunnery to half his main armament and dissipate his superior fire power; conversely, he did not wish to 'cross the T' of the enemy in the classical fashion, for by so doing he would, in the misty conditions that might reasonably be expected, reduce the duration of any engagement unless complex manoeuvres were carried out, to the detriment of accurate gunfire. Furthermore, there was the question of *Hood*'s protection: she was vulnerable to the dipping shell—a fact not disclosed to the public at large but well-known to battlecruiser commanders and admirals—and approaching an engagement beam-on, nearly parallel to the enemy, would expose his ship to plunging fire for far too long. In order to lessen the disadvantages of all his options, he therefore elected to make an interception with the enemy off his starboard bow: in this way he could close the range rapidly, minimising the time of greatest vulnerability, and also quickly bring all eighteen of his heavy guns into action.

At 2230 crews aboard *Hood*, *Prince of Wales* and the four attendant destroyers, screening ahead, were instructed to prepare for action, and at 2230 the order was given to darken ship. At 2306, *Suffolk* reported that *Bismarck* and her companion had changed course slightly, to 232°, and at 2310 Holland altered course to 285°, endeavouring to ensure that the enemy would be met on a favourable bearing. Thirty-five minutes later came a transmission from *Suffolk* indicating that the German ships had veered about 30° to port, putting them on a course of 200°; and then, at about midnight, the cruiser lost them altogether—

although naturally she did not report the problem in as many words—being able to track them neither visually nor by means of her radar because of a violent snowstorm. There was now, therefore, a distinct possibility that Lütjens, well aware of the presence of the two British cruisers and of their constant transmissions, had turned back into the narrows of the Denmark Strait to abort his sortie, fearing that British capital ships might be in the vicinity; on the other hand, the change of course may just have been a routine manoeuvre, or a deliberate attempt to shake off the shadowers. The only evidence Holland had was the change of course indicated by *Suffolk*, and so he himself altered course to 340° in response and then, five minutes later, to 000°. If both sides held to their new courses, battle could be joined much earlier than had originally been expected.

Holland slowed his squadron to 25kts and at 0015 went to action stations, with battle ensigns hoisted. At 0030 he signalled that if he had not made contact with the Germans by 0210 he would probably alter course to 180°: he must assume the worst—that the enemy was still intent on breaking through to the North Atlantic shipping lanes—and it was no good his chasing into the Arctic if the German warships passed him on their way south. In the meantime Holland hoped that *Norfolk* and *Suffolk* might regain contact.

The minutes passed. In anticipation of an imminent engagement, Holland explained to his gunnery officers that *Hood* and *Prince of Wales* should prepare to take on the *Bismarck* only; the two heavy cruisers would look after her consort *Prinz Eugen*.[10] However, he still lacked hard news. He still refused to allow the two heavy ships' radar to be switched on, insisting that the element of surprise be preserved, but *Prince of Wales*'s Walrus spotter aircraft was made ready for a reconnaissance sortie. The aircraft was to carry out a sweep to port, then describe as wide a search pattern as possible to starboard; to maximise the time aloft, the pilot was instructed to locate and land alongside one of the screening destroyers rather than make for Iceland or attempt to return to *Prince of Wales*.[11] However, the sortie was cancelled at the last moment as the weather

Right: Probably the last photograph ever taken of *Hood* as a fighting unit as she heads towards her rendezvous with *Bismarck*. As was normal practice in heavy seas or while steaming at speed, 'A' and 'B' turrets are turned away from the fore-and-aft line in order to prevent water ingress. The guns of *Prince of Wales*—from which ship the photograph was taken—are similarly trained. *Author's Collection*

suddenly closed in.[12] At 0203 Holland reached the point at which he should have made contact based on *Suffolk*'s last sighting and, as promised, turned about to a course of 200°, at the same time sending his destroyers away to the north to form a loose screen in the hope of locating the enemy. Ten minutes later he increased speed to 26kts, then at 0222 to 27kts.

Holland considered his position. His big ships were sweeping south-south-west into the Atlantic swell; his destroyers were stationed to the north, searching the horizon for signs of the enemy; *Suffolk* and *Norfolk* were to the north-west, desperately trying to regain contact with two ships they had last spotted over two hours ago; and further to the north-west was the Greenland ice-edge. *Bismarck* and *Prinz Eugen* were unlikely to be to the south of his position, but they might be to the east, closer to the Icelandic coast. To cover this eventuality, therefore, the Admiral at last ordered *Prince of Wales* to sweep his starboard quarter with her Type 284 gunnery radar. However, she was unable to comply because the equipment would not bear beyond 70°. At 0229 came the news that *Norfolk* had spotted a 'large unknown vessel', but from the plots it appeared as if this was in fact *Prince of Wales* and not one of the enemy ships.

Then, at 0247, came positive news from *Suffolk* that she had renewed contact.

DÉNOUEMENT

Bismarck and *Prinz Eugen* had been detected by *Suffolk*'s radar at a range of 19,200yds, estimated speed 28kts. The course had not, in fact changed: the two ships were still proceeding on 240°, the course indicated when Newell had first spotted them over seven hours earlier. Holland took stock once again. *Suffolk*'s report placed the enemy warships some fifteen miles to the north-west, much nearer than he had anticipated: he could close the range immediately and could bring the German ships to action within an hour or so, but he decided on a gradual approach, doubtless in the hope that visibility would improve as the day unfolded. Holland held off. His own course was 200°, diverging from that of the enemy, so at 0321 he altered 20° to starboard and twenty minutes later another 20°, bringing his ships on a course parallel with that of the enemy. He waited.

By this time a stream of W/T reports was coming in from *Suffolk*, with her sister still holding on to the wakes of the two German warships and still blissfully ignorant of the proximity of the Battle Cruiser Squadron. Holland increased speed to 28kts to maintain his position relative to the enemy; he could get an accurate fix on the two British cruisers by means of D/F interpretation and he thus had a reasonably accurate plot of where the enemy was. At 0400 the range was estimated to be twenty miles and at 0430 the visibility, continuing to improve, about twelve miles. The spotter aircraft was readied again but once more to no avail: the Walrus had been defuelled following the previous attempt at launch, and when an inspection was made of her petrol supplies it was discovered that they had become contaminated by water and it would be some time before the machine could take off. Meanwhile, for reasons unknown, at 0450 *Prince of Wales* was ordered into the van ahead of *Hood*, which fell back off her companion's port quarter; the flagship, however, resumed her position after fifteen minutes. The two British ships were ordered to take up first degree of readiness. Half an hour later, as the weather lifted, *Bismarck* and *Prinz Eugen* slid into view.

To Holland's dismay, the enemy ships were bearing 335°, approximately on the broadside, on a course of 240°, at a range of some 34,000yds, or seventeen miles; he would have wished to meet them in somewhat different circumstances, certainly further abaft the beam so that he could to some extent dictate the terms of the interception. The news of the sighting was swiftly relayed to the Admiralty and to Tovey, Commander-in-Chief Home Fleet, 'BC1' (Holland) giving his position as 63°20′N 31°50′W. Two minutes after spotting the enemy, at 0537, Holland ordered an alteration of course 40° to starboard, followed at 0549 by a further 20°. *Prince of Wales* kept her station on the flagship at 130°, off the latter's starboard quarter. Seven huge turrets swung slowly towards the north-west, gun barrels elevating in anticipation.

Lookouts on *Bismarck* and *Prinz Eugen* had sighted the British ships at almost the same time as they themselves had been seen. They were aware of approaching vessels beforehand, but they were amazed to discover that the new arrivals were capital ships—identified as *Hood* and *King George V*. Aboard *Bismarck*, Lütjens was faced with a dilemma. His orders were to locate and destroy Atlantic convoy traffic, not to engage an enemy battleship and battlecruiser. He could turn away to the north-west, but, with the ice-edge not far distant and a shadowing cruiser off his starboard quarter, he could hardly hope to escape detection for long, if at all. His route to the south-east was cut off by the approaching capital ships, and it was possible that further heavy units were not far behind. His speed would not help him either: the cruisers tracking him had held him for many hours, and he could not outrun his main opponents. He had little choice but to go into action.

Hood and *Prince of Wales* ploughed onwards, the northerly wind whipping up the seas and sending spray cascading over their forecastles, partially blinding the rangefinders. Holland was desperate to close the range as rapidly as possible, to lessen the chances of his ship being struck by plunging fire, but he could not aim his bows directly at the enemy, for to do so would enable the latter to draw ahead of him, requiring continuous, gradual changes of course to port by the Battle Cruiser Squadron—even though by approaching in this way he would be presenting the smallest possible targets to the German gunners. Instead, he had chosen to close the range more gradually, in a series of 'steps', as it were. The problem was that a rapid closing of the range was not compatible with bringing the full weight of his guns to bear: only his forward turrets would be able to fire at the enemy for the time being— until the range was short enough to risk turning *Hood* on a course parallel to that of the targets.

Holland gave the order to open fire at 0549, at a range of about 25,000yds, just after ordering the second turn to starboard. He specified that fire should be concentrated on the leading ship, bearing 337°, assuming that this would be *Bismarck*. It was not. The silhouettes of the two German warships were remarkably similar, but the Gunnery Officer aboard *Prince of Wales* noted the error and ordered the second ship to be targeted instead. The error was noted aboard *Hood* and probably rectified, though not before the first salvo had boomed out at 0552½; while the shells were in the air, *Prince of Wales* opened fire also.[13] *Hood*'s shells fell close to *Prinz Eugen*, while *Prince of Wales*'s fell long on her target. *Bismarck* replied, apparently on the orders of her Captain, Lindemann, Lütjens having remained silent. The first German 38cm salvo was short and to starboard of the British flagship. *Hood* fired again, followed once more by *Prince of Wales*. *Bismarck* returned fire, and her second salvo fell exactly between the two British ships. *Prinz Eugen* had by this time also opened fire; according to Captain Leach on *Prince of Wales*, it was his ship that the German cruiser was targeting, although according to *Prinz Eugen*'s Gunnery Officer this was not the case—his target was *Hood* also.

Bismarck's third salvo, according to most observers, straddled *Hood*, and as the shells landed a fire broke out on the shelter deck, close to the port after 4in gun mounting and spreading quickly to the base of the mainmast. Whether the fire was

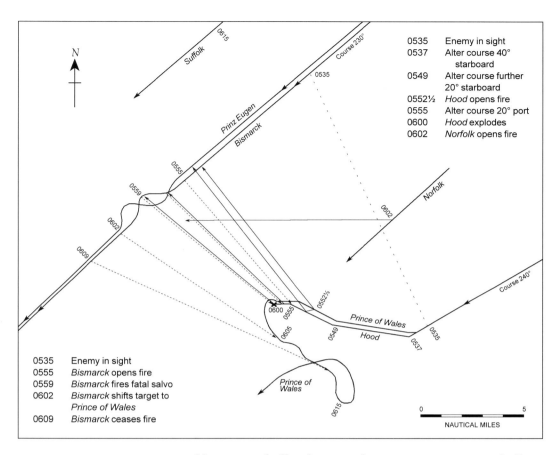

Above: The Denmark Strait—the engagement. *Author*

started by a 15in shell or by one of *Prinz Eugen*'s 20.3cm shells is a matter of contention and will never be known for certain. In any event, it was a serious affair, and the heat was so intense that it penetrated the ready-use 4in ammunition lockers and, probably, the UP missile lockers that were stowed at various places around the deck. The carnage and destruction wrought by the exploding projectiles must have been horrific. Gun crews and other personnel topside took cover as best they could, but there were many casualties.[14] Some attempt was made to extinguish the fire, but because of the havoc being caused by the explosions it was decided to wait until the ammunition had expended itself; Holland himself gave an order to this effect.

At 0555 *Hood* hoisted '2 Blue', indicating a turn 20° to port that would open her beam slightly and enable her after turrets

to be brought into action against the target. *Prince of Wales* was evidently shooting much more rapidly than the flagship, because when her own 'A' arcs were opened (i.e., when her own after turret was brought to bear following the execution of '2 Blue'), she was in the process of firing her ninth salvo; at this point *Hood* had fired only four or possibly five.[15] There is no evidence to suggest that any of *Hood*'s shells had struck the target.

The range was still coming down. At 0554 it was down to 22,000yds, at 0555 to 21,000. At about 0557, at 19,000yds, *Bis-*

marck's fourth salvo was on its way; it landed just astern of *Hood*, slightly 'over'. The range continued to decrease. *Hood*'s after turret gunlayers now had *Bismarck* in their sights and permission was given to fire; at about the same time, Holland issued a second order '2 Blue', a further turn 20° to port, which would bring his ships into a position where full broadsides could be fired. Before the turn was fully executed, *Hood* fired again, one or both or her after turrets adding their weight to the salvo fired from forward. In the meantime, the shadowing cruisers, *Norfolk* and *Suffolk*, had joined the action, but, at a range of nearly 30,000yds, their shells fell well short of the target.

At 0600 *Bismarck* fired for a fifth time, at a range of 16,500yds. Four 800kg projectiles screamed towards *Hood*, and, although they straddled, one or more of them struck the flagship. A huge column of gushing flame erupted from the shelter deck, tossing boats, gun mountings and pieces of superstructure high into the air; billowing smoke rose in a mushroom cloud. *Hood* slowed in the water, listed momentarily to starboard, righted herself and then took on an alarming list to port, exposing masses of twisted framing. The stern settled, then slipped below the waves. The bows reared up, paused for a second and then slid gently beneath the surface of the sea. As they did so, it seemed that 'A' and 'B' turret fired one last salvo towards the heavens: despite her agony, *Hood* had apparently shouted defiance even as she died.

INQUEST

HUNDREDS of pairs of eyes blinked in amazement at the spectacle just witnessed. *Hood*, the pride of the Royal Navy, symbol of Empire and the marvel of her age, had vanished: a legend had disappeared from the face of the waters. For a few seconds, minutes even, time stood still.

Then *Bismarck*'s gun roared again. *Prince of Wales*, half-way through executing the second of Holland's '2 Blue' signals, suddenly veered to starboard in order to avoid sailing through the floating debris of her flagship, temporarily throwing her gunlayers off their aim. By the time they had found it again, German shells had smashed through the battleship's compass platform. Hit after hit followed, and, with her communications disrupted and her gunnery haphazard, *Prince of Wales* made smoke and at 0613 broke off the action, turning away to the south. She had fired eighteen salvos altogether, and observers on board were doubtful whether any hits had been made.

They were wrong: three 14in shells had struck *Bismarck*, one of them causing a serious oil leak and obliging Lütjens to abandon his plans for 'Rheinübung'. He decided to make for France, allowing *Prinz Eugen* to proceed on her own in search of convoys. Feinting a change of course, he turned upon his pursuers and opened fire to enable his consort to escape, and so began a game of cat-and-mouse which has become a classic in the annals of naval history. First, in the evening of 24 May,

Swordfish torpedo-bombers from *Victorious*, which had been detached with four cruisers from Tovey in his flagship *King George V*, were launched against her, scoring one torpedo hit but causing no damage. Then, the next day, contact was lost. It was not regained until 26 May, by a Catalina flying boat of Coastal Command. Meanwhile Force 'H', coming up from Gibraltar with *Renown*, the carrier *Ark Royal*, the cruiser *Sheffield* and destroyers, manoeuvred into position, and late that day *Sheffield* gained contact and took up a shadowing position. Swordfish from *Ark Royal* were launched, and, after a fortunately abortive attack in error on *Sheffield*, succeeded in striking the German battleship's stern, jamming her steering gear. Now describing large circles, *Bismarck* could only await her inevitable doom. The following morning, after a night spent warding off destroyer torpedo attacks, she was hammered into a blazing hulk by the battleships *King George V* and *Rodney*, the latter detached from convoy escort duties, and she sank beneath the Atlantic after an action lasting two hours, torpedoed by the cruiser *Dorsetshire*.[1]

FIRST INQUIRY

At 2100 on 24 May 1941 the Admiralty issued a solemn communiqué: 'British naval forces intercepted early this morning, off the coast of Greenland, German naval forces, including the battleship *Bismarck*. The enemy were attacked, and during the ensuing action HMS *Hood* . . . received an unlucky hit in the magazine and blew up. . . . It is feared there will be few survivors from HMS *Hood*.' There were, in fact only three, out of a complement of 1,418. Plainly, some investigation into the disaster was required, and the wheels were set in motion very quickly.

On 28 May the First Lord of the Admiralty, Sir Dudley Pound, wrote to the Controller noting the 'disturbing' nature of the disaster, expressing his concern that *Hood*'s loss appeared 'to the onlooker' to bear remarkable similarities to the losses of three battlecruisers at Jutland, and urging that the 'whole matter, going back to the records of the last war', be re-examined. The Controller replied two days later in a

positive spirit, although he did not think that a magazine explosion was responsible on this occasion.

A Board of Inquiry was set up on Friday 30 May and convened the following day. Presiding was Vice-Admiral Sir Geoffrey Blake, and also on the Board were Captain C. F. Hammill (HMS *President*) and Captain C. H. J. Harcourt (HMS *Duke of York*). Few witnesses were called—eight from *Prince of Wales* and eight from *Norfolk*; surprisingly, only one of *Hood*'s three survivors was required to give evidence. Although reports of the entire action involving the Battle Cruiser Squadron and the two German warships were given by the witnesses, most interest centred on two events—the fire on *Hood*'s shelter deck and the subsequent massive explosion.

The witnesses more or less agreed on the location and cause of the first. Rear-Admiral Wake-Walker and Lieutenant Viscount Kelburn, his Flag Lieutenant aboard *Norfolk*, observed 'a glow aft . . . in the neighbourhood of the mainmast'; pink in colour, it later 'spread forward . . . eventually covering the middle of the ship'. Commander Luce, on *Norfolk*'s flag deck, saw 'a glow as a cordite fire, between the mainmast and "X" turret', while Lieutenant Royds saw the fire start 'at the foot of the mainmast' and considered that it was cordite burning; Lieutenant Langford also saw 'a cordite fire'. Yeoman Tonkin said that it looked like 'a wood fire'. *Norfolk*'s Captain, A. J. L. Phillips, saw something different—'a brilliant flash under the after funnel'—while Chief Yeoman Mighall saw 'a tower of flame'. Most of the witnesses aboard *Norfolk* agreed that the fire quickly subsided.

Captain Leach, on board *Prince of Wales*, had a closer view: he was only about 1,000yds distant from his flagship during the action whereas *Norfolk* was some 30,000yds away. He pinpointed the fire as starting on the 'port side of the after superstructure', close to the after 4in mounting, and stated that it was confined to the port side of the shelter deck (i.e., the disengaged side). His colleague Lieutenant R. C Beckwith identified the flames as a cordite fire, described by Lieutenant-Commander Terry as 'deep red' with 'heavy black smoke' in contrast to Sub-Lieutenant Wormsley, who saw yellow flames. Chief Petty Officer French also saw a cordite fire. Midshipman Dundas, one of the three survivors from *Hood*, described how the Torpedo Officer reported a 'cordite fire'. There was general agreement that it had been *Bismarck*'s third salvo which was responsible for the conflagration.

There was less of a consensus of opinion about the fatal hit or hits. From his distant vantage point, Wake-Walker saw a mushroom-shaped explosion, followed by a 'red glow' and a trail of black smoke drifting to leeward (that is, to the south); his Captain estimated the explosion as being of the order of 600 to 700ft (in height, presumably). Luce stated that there was 'a big flash, higher than the mainmast', while Mighall witnessed 'a large cone' (presumably inverted). Leach saw 'a funnel of flame . . . double the height of the [main]mast' and with a base diameter of 20–30ft. Terry estimated the height of the explosion to be 200ft, spreading to a mushroom shape; Wormsley saw a large yellow flash 'higher than the mast'. As to the seat of the detonation, Wake-Walker and Kelburn pointed to 'the centre of the ship'. Luce thought that it was from 'X' magazine but might have been 'as far forward as the mainmast'; Mighall pinpointed the location as 'abreast the after turrets'; and Tonkin stated that the 'sixth [*sic*] salvo caused fire fore and aft . . . and an explosion which came from the funnels aft'. On board *Prince of Wales*, the Captain saw the explosion emanating from between the after funnel and the mainmast, with which opinion Beckwith agreed. Terry indicated that the explosion erupted from the vicinity of 'X' turret, and testified that he saw some of the ship's frames as she heeled over. Other observers saw differently: French saw flames coming from under the water and run along *Hood*'s waterline, while Chief Ordnance Artificer Westlake claimed to have seen shells strike the flagship amidships at the waterline and plating being blown away shortly thereafter. Dundas, who of course had the closest encounter of all the witnesses, remembered wreckage falling but, being on the upper bridge at the time, had no clear view of the event. Several of the witnesses on board *Prince of Wales*, and Dundas, remarked upon the quietness of the explosion: there had been 'no great noise,' said one.

Within but a few days, on 2 June, the Board of Inquiry submitted its findings in the form of a short report. It concluded that *Bismarck*'s third salvo had struck *Hood* near P2 4in mounting, causing a cordite fire amongst the ready-use ammunition. The fact that it spread, flared up and then died down was noted. Captain Phillips's opinion that warheads associated with the upper-deck torpedo tubes had exploded was dismissed. As to the main explosion, this was centred at about the base of the mainmast, variations from this location given by observers being attributable, perhaps, to the differing angles and distances from the scene. One or more shells from *Bismarck* directly penetrated *Hood*'s protection, causing the after magazines to explode, and the fact that the nearest magazine to the base of the mainmast (the 4in magazine) was 65ft away could be explained by a venting of the explosion through the 'after engine room'. The explosion of the 4in magazine would probably have caused the adjacent 15in magazines to blow up. The cordite fire that appeared after the enemy's third salvo did not cause the loss of the ship.

Considering the gravity of the matter, many of its readers regarded the report as at best rushed and superficial and at worst erroneous in its conclusions. In particular, the Director

Below: A minute or so after *Hood* blows up a pall of smoke hangs over the Atlantic to mark the demise of the British battlecruiser. *Prince of Wales* had to make violent manoeuvres in order to avoid the wreckage. *Gerhard Koop Collection*

of Naval Construction, Sir Stanley Goodall, was less than impressed. He contended that, although the 4in magazines could have set off the adjacent main 15in magazines, the shell or shells which caused the primary detonation, had they struck the 4in magazine directly, would have had to have fuses with an extraordinarily long delay, particularly if those witnesses who claimed that the shells struck an area near the mainmast were correct in their opinions. Furthermore, had the main 15in magazines exploded, 'the structure above [that is, the extreme after end of the shelter deck and 'Y' and 'X' turrets] would have been entirely destroyed'; this was not, apparently, the case. He observed that the Board had offered no evidence as to the reason why a magazine explosion might travel horizontally, towards the area of the engine rooms—and the centre engine room at that—before venting upwards through the shelter deck. The reason for the loss of the ship, he suggested, might actually be that which Captain Phillips had put forward—the simultaneous explosion of *Hood*'s torpedo warheads.[2] Finally, Goodall urged that consideration be given to holding a much more thoroughgoing investigation, to include the views of explosives experts and the recollections of survivors from *Bismarck*. Vice-Admiral Sir Tom Phillips, Pound's deputy, expressed his disgust at the way in which the Board of Inquiry had been conducted and recommended the con-

vening of a second Board, in which all material witnesses would be called, further evidence taken and a full record kept. Pound himself concurred, as did Admiral Tovey, Commander-in-Chief Home Fleet.

SECOND INQUIRY

The second Board of Inquiry convened on 27 August, three months after *Hood*'s loss, under the presidency of Admiral H. T. C. Walker, the ship's captain of a few years previously. The other members were Captains H. E. Morse and L. D. Mackintosh. The opinions of experts in construction and ordnance were solicited, witnesses from *Prince of Wales*, *Norfolk* and *Suffolk* were summoned, and also giving evidence were the two survivors from *Hood* who had not taken part in the first Inquiry and a number of crew members from *Bismarck*.

Most of the witnesses from the British ships confirmed, in broad terms, what had been said at the first Inquiry. Captain Leach described the first fire as being 'irregular and flickering' and 'about twelve or fourteen feet high'; Rear-Admiral Wake-Walker stated that it was a 'brilliant rose colour'. Other witnesses aboard *Norfolk* saw 'balls of fire showing clearly in the flame of the explosion'. Robert Tilburn, one of the survivors from *Hood*, was on the disengaged side of the ship during the action and indicated that the first fire appeared to have been

Below: Inboard profile of *Hood*, 1941, Stations 175–352. *Author*

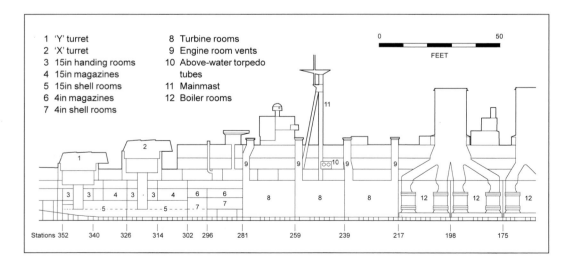

1 'Y' turret
2 'X' turret
3 15in handling rooms
4 15in magazines
5 15in shell rooms
6 4in magazines
7 4in shell rooms
8 Turbine rooms
9 Engine room vents
10 Above-water torpedo tubes
11 Mainmast
12 Boiler rooms

0   50
FEET

Stations 352   340   326   314   302   296   281   259   239   217   198   175

the result of a single hit that burst on the shelter deck, setting off UP ammunition, not only in the lockers but also ready loaded in the projectors themselves. Ordinary Signalman Briggs, the third survivor, was on the compass platform during the engagement and was therefore in a position to hear the comments of some of the senior officers as the action unfolded; he told the Inquiry that the Squadron Gunnery Officer indicated that the fire had started in the ready-use lockers, without mentioning whether they were 4in or UP. The hit had been made, said Briggs, on the starboard side; this contradicted Leach's testimony that it had occurred on the port side of the ship.

As to the fatal explosion, Leach elaborated a little, describing 'a very fierce upward rush of flame the shape of a . . . thin funnel . . . giving the impression of a vast blow lamp'. He did not hear any noise. He thought that *Hood*'s two after turrets were 'widely separated from the explosion'. Commander L. E. Porter, on board *Suffolk* during the action, saw 'a very thin, parallel-sided pillar of orange flame . . . followed by a cloud of very dark smoke . . .' Tilburn, remarkably, did not see anything of the detonation, recalling only 'a tremendous vibration' and falling debris. One of Leach's colleagues on board *Prince of Wales*, Petty Officer Sweet, stated that the stern of the ship was 'blown to pieces'; several others remarked on the fact that sections of main turrets had been catapulted into the air. Lieutenant-Commander Terry noted that 'the after part of the ship was a mass of twisted framework'. Briggs confirmed that, after the explosion, the ship had first listed to starboard, then righted herself, and then heeled violently to port. He saw the bows standing vertically in the water as he swam away. Tilburn confirmed this impression: he had noticed the fore part of the ship, from the after funnel forward, 'well out of the water'. When he was in the water he also noticed, amongst the detritus, a mass of 'steel tubes, sealed at both ends'—doubtless crushing tubes from her bulges. Everybody agreed that *Hood* sank within three minutes; from the evidence of both the British sailors and the German prisoners from *Bismarck*, it was clear that she broke her back.

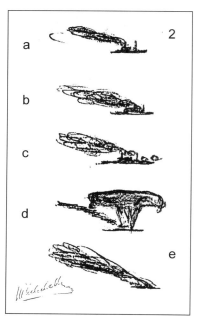

Left: The loss of HMS *Hood*, as sketched by three of the principal witnesses:
1. Sketches produced for the first Board of Inquiry by Captain John Leach of *Prince of Wales*. His ship was at a distance of four cables (810yds) when the explosion occurred.
2. Sketches drawn by Rear-Admiral W. F. Wake-Walker as seen from *Norfolk* 'approximately ten miles away'. The sketches are annotated as follows: (a) 'Fire, a small glow.' (b) 'Glow increases and spreads horizontally.' (c) 'Glow dies down. Fore turrets fire.' (d) 'Ship blows up.' (e) 'Slight red glow on surface and smoke.' A further note to the sketches indicates that 'there was no pall of smoke over the explosion; all smoke was streaming away to leeward'.
3. Annotated sketches by Captain A. J. L Phillips, also on board *Norfolk*. The annotations read (a) 'Heavy splash of flame here'; (b) 'Smoke'; (c) 'Pulsating fire, probably cordite'; and (d) 'Grey smoke', 'Splash' and 'Ball of brilliant fire ascending rapidly'. *Crown Copyright*

A great deal of technical evidence was extracted from the various experts who had been called to the Inquiry, particularly concerning the possibility that *Hood*'s torpedo warheads had detonated, the characteristics of the German 38cm shell, the possibility of *Hood*'s magazines having been directly penetrated and the comparative characteristics of cordite fires and TNT explosions. Among those whose opinion was sought were representatives of the Director of Naval Ordnance, the Director of Torpedoes and Mining and the Chief Scientist of the Research Department of the Admiralty. It was generally agreed that a bursting shell could have set off torpedo warheads, though no more than two of them, and the subsequent explosion would not have in its turn set off the ship's main magazines. There would, however, according to Goodall's representative, have been sufficient damage to the structure of the ship to cause her to sink, though not all the experts agreed on this point. Had the warheads indeed exploded, then there would have been an instantaneous bright flash, lighter in colour than a cordite fire.

With regard to the characteristics of German shells, there was general consensus that if their muzzle velocity was more than 3,050fs, then one could have penetrated *Hood*'s main 12in belt; if some 300fs lower, then it could not have penetrated the main belt but may have been able to enter the ship's vitals by striking a strip of the upper 7in belt at such an angle that it could have passed beneath the main protective deck.[3] There was also the possibility that a shell could have entered the ship below the main belt, travelling underwater before it did so. All these theories, however, assumed an extraordinarily long fuse delay.[4]

In more general terms, the Board observed that the fire arising from *Bismarck*'s third salvo first appeared on the port side abaft the mainmast and that it spread very rapidly but probably only laterally and not below decks. It could have been caused either by petrol (unlikely) or by the ignition of ready-use 4in or UP ammunition (much more likely). However, this fire would not have brought about the destruction of the ship: moreover, there was little likelihood of the fire flashing down into the 4in magazine because it was virtually certain that all the hatches would have been closed. The detonation of torpedo warheads was possible, but there was no 'direct evidence' that this was what had in fact taken place; nor would it have produced the huge column of flame seen by almost all distant observers; and it would have produced much more noise than was heard by those close to the event. The DNC's representative and Chief Constructor, D. E. J. Offord, dissented from the general view in that he felt that such a detonation could have caused the loss of the ship, but the damage to the stern observed by witnesses appeared to be much more extensive than would have been caused by a detonation of this nature.

However, what actually was observed was compatible with the blowing up of one or more of the 4in or 15in magazines or both; and an explosion in the 4in magazines would almost certainly set off the 15in magazines. There remained the location of the explosion, which, it was generally agreed, was just forward of the mainmast; this could be explained by the fact that, if the 4in magazines exploded first, followed a split second later by the 15in magazine(s), then the egress of the explosion could well have been just forward of the former; in any case, the Board's report went on, the path followed by the detonation of over 100 tons of cordite would be 'difficult to predict'. Finally, the effects witnessed were by all accounts very similar to those seen when the three battlecruisers blew up at Jutland.

The conclusions of the Board were that (a) the loss could be ascribed to a hit from a 38cm shell in or near to a 4in or 15in magazine, causing them all to explode; (b) *Hood*'s torpedo warheads may or may not have exploded, but such could not in any event have caused the loss of the ship; and (c) the earlier fire on the shelter deck involved the detonation of ready-use 4in or UP ammunition, or both, but did not contribute to the loss of the ship.

AFTERMATH

The findings of the second Board of Inquiry, then, though more detailed than those of the first, more or less repeated what had been arrived at previously. What the Inquiry did not address—and, of course, could not—was this question: at what point on the ship did the fatal shell strike, and at what trajectory? In other words, was it the ship's vertical armour that was deficient, or her horizontal armour? These and other questions were debated for many months afterwards, for, although *Hood* was a unique warship, there were, plainly, lessons to be learned that would benefit the rest of the Fleet. Were the magazines of other ships—especially capital ships—

adequately protected? Were they truly flash-tight? Was there any way in which the cordite charges necessary to fire heavy shells could be made safer? Could loading drills be improved in the interests of greater safety? And, with regard to the shelter deck fire—which may or may not have had an influence on the final catastrophe—was it absolutely necessary to stow medium-calibre ammunition adjacent to the mountings?

It was, in many ways, Jutland revisited, and most of the questions had been tackled in the 1920s following the disasters there. Extensive trials had been conducted, and, because nobody had quite gone as far as deliberately blowing up a battleship, there was a great deal of theory available but little hard evidence. For example, venting arrangements were improved as a result of these trials, encouraging the blast from a cordite explosion to dissipate upwards rather than flash downwards towards the magazine; it was recommended that improved flash-tight doors be introduced between shell rooms and handing rooms, and between the handing rooms and the ammunition hoists; and handing rooms were introduced where they previously had not existed, that is, for hand-loaded secondary batteries. The cordite charges also came in for criticism. Whereas charges for quick-firing guns—as were *Hood*'s 4in twins—were kept in brass casings, those for the main armament were enclosed in silk bags and therefore much more likely to take fire; furthermore, the powder igniters for the charges were contained within the cartridges themselves instead of being stowed separately in flashtight brass containers.[5]

Although much was done between the wars to implement the recommendations made as a result of the Jutland disasters, the changes made were generally confined to guns of 8in calibre and below—in other words, to the main armament of cruisers and the secondary armament only of capital ships. The difficulty was that all the heavy ships, with the exception of *Hood*, pre-dated Jutland, and even *Hood* pre-dated the findings of the Jutland post-mortems: it was simply too expensive in the frugal days following the Great War to contemplate introducing such wide-ranging measures. Even in

Nelson and *Rodney*, completed in 1927, bagged cordite charges were retained because trials with other types of cases had shown up major disadvantages.

The other major topic for debate concerned horizontal protection. The obvious first point was that the magazines in *Hood* were situated above the shell rooms; thus a plunging projectile, if it penetrated the horizontal protective plating, would burst directly in the magazine rather than in the (relatively) safer environment of the shell room, the contents of which might fracture or break but not explode. The reason magazines were situated above shell rooms was generally a logistical one: gun-loading arrangements were simplified in this manner, and, as we have seen, it was not possible to modify the design after the ship had been laid down, despite the voices raised in criticism. As to the form of the ship's horizontal protection, it was realised very early in the building process that *Hood* was deficient in this respect, and additional plating was worked in. However, subsequent trials with new armour-piercing shells demonstrated that these modifications were quite inadequate: in fact, in 1918 a mock target representing *Hood*'s level of protection was set up, and it was discovered that a 15in shell could penetrate the ship's magazines with ease. Although promises were made at official level that the ship would in due course be fitted with up to 5in of face-hardened armour plate over her magazines, these promises could not be fulfilled. Doubtless the work would have been carried out had the ship been reconstructed as planned beginning in 1939.

Action taken as a direct consequence of the loss of *Hood* included approval to fit an additional 2in of armour over the magazines of the remaining *Royal Sovereign* class battleships, which, with the advent of hostilities, would of course not now be scrapped on the commissioning of the *King George V*s, as was originally planned; *Revenge* never received this extra armour and on *Ramillies* the work was begun but never completed, although *Resolution* and *Royal Sovereign* herself were modified to the standards called for. It was also approved to fit an armoured bulkhead forward from the hold to the platform deck in *Nelson* and *Rodney* and, in the latter ship, to fit additional lower deck armour as already introduced into her sister-ship, but, owing to other, more pressing demands on the dockyards, these recommendations were never implemented. As regards the *Queen Elizabeth*s, it was agreed that an armoured bulkhead forward be fitted and the horizontal armour over the magazines be extended, but it is believed that, again, these modifications were never made. *Renown* was the only remaining capital ship with above-water torpedo tubes, and in the light of the *Hood* disaster these were ordered to be removed; however, for some reason, only four of her eight tubes were landed. One recommendation that was swiftly implemented was the removal of the hated UP mountings, which in 1941 adorned many of the Royal Navy's capital ships and cruisers. As to the problem of ready-use lockers, the dangers were emphasised but the risk was accepted, especially since anti-aircraft weapons on board ship had begun to proliferate in the light of war experience.

The two Boards of Inquiry exonerated Vice-Admiral Holland from any culpability regarding the loss of his ship, but, inevitably, post-war analysts have questioned his tactics. Much has been made of the fact that he entered the engagement head to the wind, with spray drenching his rangefinders and with only about half his firepower available because both *Hood*'s and *Prince of Wales*'s after turrets could not bear. However, he had little choice but to approach from the direction he did, and, once the enemy had been sighted, he was doubtless anxious to close the range as fast as possible so

Right: Approximate relative positions of *Hood* and *Prince of Wales* at the start of the engagement with *Bismarck* and *Prinz Eugen*. Author (redrawn from ADM1164531)

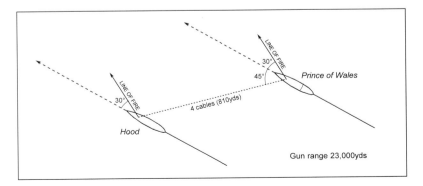

as to lessen the chances of a dipping shell striking his ship's decks. Once the range was down, he gave orders for two separate turns to port so as to open his 'A' arcs. It was while the second of these turns was being executed, or immediately after it had been completed, that *Hood* exploded. Holland's tactic of choosing battle with his ships in close formation has also been criticised; *Prince of Wales* was only four cables distant—in layman's terms less than three *Hood*'s lengths away—and this enabled *Bismarck* to switch her fire to the battleship following the loss of the flagship. While this argument—which is a criticism of contemporary Admiralty battle orders as much as of Holland—doubtless has merit in that two separated targets are more difficult to engage than two close targets, it hardly explains why *Hood* was sunk. Again, the Admiral has been taken to task for misidentifying his target, and it is true that this error was made and, indeed, may never have been corrected aboard the flagship; but while the criticism is valid and may be evidence of an officer with short-comings, it does not explain why the world's largest battle-cruiser suddenly disappeared from the face of the ocean.[6] One might as well argue that had *Hood* been in a different place when the fatal shell landed she would not have been lost.

An extraordinary amount of speculation surrounds the loss of *Hood*, and this speculation continues sixty years after the event; it will doubtless continue well into the future. Eminent theorists have produced masses of computer models, data and

Below: Approximate relative positions of *Hood* and *Prince of Wales* as the engagement with *Bismarck* and *Prinz Eugen* unfolded. *Author*

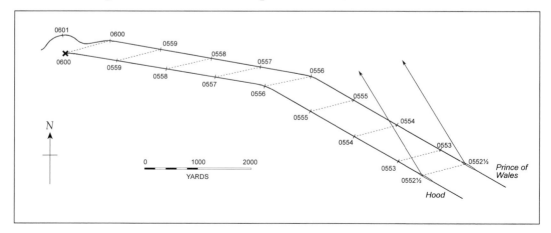

Above: A painting by J. C. Schmitz-Westerholt, showing *Hood* sinking following the catastrophic explosion. HMS *Prince of Wales* is in the foreground. Purists will note inaccuracies in the physiognomy of the ships, but the drama of the event is imaginatively rendered. *US Naval Historical Center*

diagrams involving range charts, the descent patterns of shells of a certain calibre and velocity, calculations of angles of obliquity and the probability of projectiles penetrating armour at various angles of inclination; at the other end of the scale some bizarre explanations have been put forward, including the Royal Navy's use of unsuitable gunpowder (*sic*).

The truth will probably never be known. It is likely that it was the explosion of her 15in after magazines that caused *Hood*'s loss. How this was brought about—whether from a direct hit, penetrating horizontal or vertical armour or passing through an unprotected point; whether from a direct hit in the adjacent 4in magazines, which exploded and set off the main magazines; whether from the detonation of the ship's torpedo warheads, again setting off the magazines; whether from a trail of combustion arising out of the fire on the shelter deck; whether from an accident, of whatever character, in one of the turrets, handing rooms or magazines—may forever remain a mystery. One thing is certain, however: the like of HMS *Hood* was not seen before nor ever will be again.

EPILOGUE

FOR SIXTY YEARS the wreck of the battlecruiser *Hood* has been lying at the bottom of the Denmark Strait, position approximately 63°22'N 32°00'W, the silent tomb for hundreds of British sailors who perished on that grey Empire Day morning in 1941. The ship had gone, but she was not forgotten.

Former crew members had kept in touch over the years, but in 1975 contacts were placed on a more organised basis with the formation of the HMS Hood Association, whose members now include veterans, veterans' families, the families of the crew members who died when the ship went down, and other interested individuals. The activities of the Association include and annual AGM and dinner, a Remembrance Day ceremony at the Southsea Memorial in Portsmouth, and an annual Memorial Service at the Church of St John the Baptist at Boldre in Hampshire. This last was the church at which Hood's last admiral, Lancelot Holland, worshipped, and after the war his widow Phyllis arranged for various memorabilia to be

Below: The church of St John the Baptist at Boldre in Hampshire.

176

held within its walls. The mementoes now include Books of Remembrance, a framed photograph of the ship, a handsome painting, a small stained glass window and several facsimiles of the ship' badge; the Memorial Services are held on the Sunday nearest to 24 May.

At the Association's annual reunion in May 1995, members were introduced to David Mearns, one of the world's leading experts on the deep-sea investigation and recovery of sunken ships and whose successes had recently included the location and investigation of the remains of the bulk carrier *Derbyshire* off Okinawa. Plans were mooted for an expedition (involving Independent Television News[1]) not only to locate but also to film the wreck of *Hood*.

With the blessing of the Association, the Ministry of Defence, the Royal British Legion and the Commonwealth War Graves Commission—and after many months of research into the records and archives in order to familiarise themselves with the physical appearance of the battlecruiser, to identify the best weather conditions for the search and to study the geomorphology of the sea bed and current patterns in the Denmark Strait—David Mearns' Blue Water Recoveries team arrived over the likely approximate position of the wreck on 17 July 2001.[2] The headquarters ship was the survey vessel *Northern Horizon*, a former deep-sea trawler, equipped with sensors to enable her to determine her position with reference to a navigational satellite and to hold the position with extreme accuracy by means of computer-controlled adjustments, taking into account wind and sea conditions.

The most important pieces of apparatus on board were the Ocean Explorer 6000 Remotely Operated Vehicle (ROV), equipped with sophisticated low-frequency side-scan sonar, which, towed behind the mother ship, would conduct sweeps of the sea bed and send back images to the interpretation team on the surface; the Magellan 725 ROV, equipped with high-technology lights and cameras, to film the remains once they had been located; and a SeaCast satellite communications system, which would enable live video pictures to be transmitted to a television studio in London.

Parts of the wreck were first tentatively identified on 20 July, and it was quickly obvious that the damage sustained by the ship in that final terrifying explosion was more horrific than had hitherto been thought. By the time the investigation closed it had been discovered that the hull had broken into three substantial portions, not two as had been the received wisdom prior to the expedition. There was a 100ft long stern section, from the ensign staff forward as far as 'Y' barbette, the aftermost quarterdeck, its teak planking preserved in remarkably fine condition, standing eerily almost upright and the remainder lying flat on the sea bed, fractured presumably as a result of the impact when it hit the bottom; a 350ft centre section, extending from approximately 'A' barbette to Station 239 (i.e., to the after bulkhead of the forwardmost turbine room), lying inverted and semi-buried in silt; and a 100ft bow section, from the forepeak as far aft as the main capstans, lying on its port side and missing most of its internal structure. Some 300ft of the hull was therefore absent, a huge midships section forward from 'Y' barbette and a short section of the bow immediately forward of 'A' barbette. The former was to be expected—the violent explosion which caused *Hood*'s loss, characterised by a huge pillar of flame seen to shoot up into the sky from the region of the mainmast, was the one certain fact testified to by all the eye-witnesses present back in May 1941—but the latter came as something of a surprise. One of two explanations is possible: the damage was caused by implosion due to the enormous water pressure found at these depths; or there was a secondary major explosion, possibly involving the forward magazines, as the ship went down. The evidence for the latter is quite strong: there is the fact that the interior

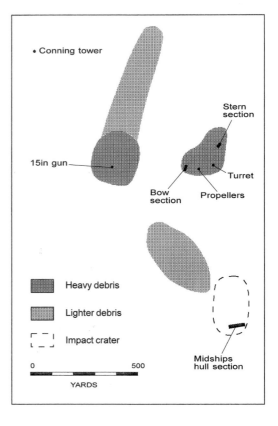

Below: Approximate disposition of *Hood*'s wreckage, the density of the debris in two areas being particularly heavy—evidence of the enormity of the explosion. The depth of the water here is just over 9,000ft. *Author*

Above: *Hood*'s bow section lies on its port side, anchor cables drooping from the foredeck. The degaussing cable along the starboard side can be clearly seen. *David Mearns/Blue Water Recoveries*

of the bow section is almost bereft of structure; there is the missing section of bow from 'A' barbette to the fore-deck; the main armour belt on the starboard side of the large midships section of the ship has been blown away and, moreover, this section shows areas of plating curling outwards at its forward break point; and the 600-ton conning tower and various components of the bridge structure were located over a mile away from the midships section of the hull.

A theory now emerges: as was speculated at both Boards of Inquiry, the detonation of the after main magazines by a shell from *Bismarck* almost certainly vented forward through the turbine rooms, the flames following the lines of least resistance and shooting upwards through the turbine room vents. However, it now seems reasonable to speculate that the pressure and flames from the explosion also travelled well forward through the hull, perhaps reaching and detonating the forward magazines too, tossing parts of the forward superstructure well clear of the hull. This is entirely consistent with the testimony during the first Board of Inquiry of Chief Petty Officer French, who claimed to have seen, from his vantage point on board *Prince of Wales*, flames travelling forward along *Hood*'s hull at the waterline, and with that of two of the survivors, who observed fire around the forward superstructure shortly after the detonation aft; it may also explain the appearance of flames shooting out of the forward main guns just as the bows reared in the air. There is less evidence concerning other theories as to what caused the loss of *Hood*. For example, the question of whether her torpedo warheads exploded cannot, for the moment, be confirmed, although it seems unlikely that all remained intact during the conflagration. If they did detonate, their contribution to the disaster cannot be evaluated, even though the after portion of one torpedo was discovered in the wreckage on the sea bed. Neither can the effect of the shelter-deck fire that erupted prior to the main explosion be calculated. It is of course entirely possible that further study of the video footage captured during Magellan's wan-

Above: *Hood's* conning tower, discovered over a mile away from the midships section of the wreck. *David Mearns/Blue Water Recoveries*

derings around the debris will give a better indication of what exactly happened on that fateful day. One argument has, however, almost certainly been settled: *Hood's* rudder is angled 20° to port, suggesting that Holland's second '2 Blue' order was indeed being executed when his ship was struck.

A great deal of other wreckage litters the sea bed where *Hood* went down—a condenser has been identified, as have a considerable portion of the mainmast, components of the main armament, parts of the bridge superstructure and what appear to be sections of the after superstructure. More poignant artefacts have also been noticed—one of the ship's bells, a teapot, and a seaman's boot.

After six days of exploration, during which four dives were made by Magellan, the final task for the Blue Water Recoveries team was to arrange for the laying of a bronze plaque of remembrance, incorporating a compact disc bearing the names of those who died, close to the bow section of the wreck, followed by a brief memorial service and the placing of a wreath on the waters of the Denmark Strait. Entirely appropriately, the ceremonies were performed by Ted Briggs, the only man still alive to have witnessed, on board, the loss of the Royal Navy's 'Mighty *Hood*'.

NOTES

Chapter 1

1. In the 1903 edition of *Jane's Fighting Ships* Cuniberti published his plans for a fast battleship with twelve 12in guns—which no doubt concentrated the Committee's minds in their planning of *Dreadnought*.

2. In Royal Navy warships, main turrets were identified by means of the letters 'A' (forward), 'B' (superfiring forward), 'Y' (aftermost) and 'X' (superfiring aft). Single main turrets amidships were designated 'Q', two amidships arranged for cross-deck firing being designated 'P' (port) and 'Q' (starboard).

3. The officer was Major F. W. Harvey, a Royal Marine, who was awarded a posthumous Victoria Cross for his gallantry.

4. Jellicoe implies as much: 'Inquiry into this matter [i.e. the loss of the battlecruisers] showed that one explanation was that our ships were very inadequately protected by armour as compared with the German vessels of the battle cruiser type. It was considered undesirable to draw attention to this publicly while the War was in progress.' (Jellicoe, p. 307)

5. Parkes is quite adamant on this point: 'The fact that our propellant cordite exploded when exposed to flash in the magazines explains the loss of the battle cruisers . . .' (Parkes, p. 640). The loss in July 1917 of the battleship *Vanguard* to spontaneous explosion when the ship was at anchor in Scapa Flow seemed to provide further evidence of the instability of British cordite.

6. Preston, pp. 155–6.

Chapter 2

1. In fact, the *Mackenen*s were to be armed with 14in guns, but the 15in weapon was known to

be under development for the *Bayern* class battleships and it was assumed that the larger calibre would be adopted for the new battle-cruisers.

2. It has long been held that the first keel plates were laid on the slipway for Ship No 460 on 31 May 1916, even as the Grand Fleet was under way in the North Sea to do battle with the High Seas Fleet. However, no primary evidence to support this claim has yet been found.

3. *Renown* and *Repulse* were nearing completion at the time, having been laid down only sixteen months beforehand. However, this rate of building was unusually fast, 2½ years from keel-laying to completion being more typical for a capital ship.

4. The principles held for other types of warship, too, although greater flexibility with regard to armour was available because other factors (for example, speed, manoeuvrability, small size) provided an element of protection in themselves.

5. Horizontal (deck) armour was more correctly referred to as 'protective plating': it was not face-hardened as was true armour plate.

6. In his 'Reflections on the Battle of Jutland', Jellicoe concentrates almost exclusively on the threat to the Grand Fleet posed by German torpedo-boats: 'It had excited more attention in the two or three years before the War than any other question of tactics . . .' Battlecruisers, by contrast, are barely mentioned. (Jellicoe, pp 392–417)

7. The forecastle deck encompassed not only the forecastle of the ship proper: the deck level might continue well aft of amidships, but it was still referred to as the forecastle deck.

8. Some of *Hood*'s 5.5in guns are still in existence. During 1941 two of them were set up at Fort

Bedford, overlooking Georgetown on Ascension Island. They were brought into action later that year when *U 124* closed the island, hoping to sink a ship or shell the cable station, and succeeded in driving the intruder away. The guns were restored by RAF personnel in the 1980s and are now looked after by the Ascension Island Historical Society. An unshielded 5.5in gun from *Hood* can also seen at the entrance to Tórshavn Harbour in the Faröe Islands.

9. His views were based on tests undertaken at the Admiralty Experimental Works at Haslar, which showed that mines tended to be washed aside by the bow waves but then 'sucked in' towards the ship as the hull passed by.

10. These torpedo tubes would become the source of much anguish. See Chapter 6.

11. However, the ship had been named not after Sir Horace Hood but after Lord Samuel Hood (First Viscount Hood of Whitley) (1724–1816), Commander-in Chief of the North American Station, Commander-in-Chief of the Mediterranean Station who occupied Toulon and captured Corsica, and briefly Member of Parliament for Westminster.

12. A good deal of confusion surrounds the official cancellation dates of *Hood*'s sister-ships. Some sources quote March 1917, although in fact this was merely one of the occasions when the Board of Admiralty informed the three builders of the low priority which was to be given to the ships. Other sources quote 27 February 1919 (as the day the Board agreed their 'final' decision) and 17 March 1919 (the date on which letters informing the builders of the Board's wishes were apparently despatched). However, it seems clear that the decision to cancel was taken in principle immediately the Armistice came into effect.

Chapter 3

1. *Hood* was the last battlecruiser completed for the Royal Navy but she and her sister-ships were not the last to be ordered. The design for a class of four new ships was completed in autumn 1921 and orders were placed on 26 October that year, a fortnight or so before the opening of the Washington Naval Conference. Their dimensions were comparable to those of *Hood*, but these 48,400-ton ships would have mounted nine 16in guns in triple turrets and have had a considerably more comprehensive armour scheme. The ships are usually referred to as the 'G3' class after their design reference, although it has been suggested that the names *Invincible*, *Inflexible*, *Indomitable* and *Indefatigable* had been earmarked. However, the Treasury vetoed them, work was suspended as the Washington Conference got under way and the contracts were cancelled soon afterwards.

2. These became *Nelson* and *Rodney*, completed in 1927 within the Washington restrictions.

3. Da Gama actually died in 1524 in India, but his remains were not interred in his home country until the following year.

4. Taylor, p. 298.

5. In his childhood, James had been the model for 'Bubbles', whose picture adorned advertisements across the country for Pear's soap. The nickname endured.

6. There had apparently been some confusion between the two navigating officers concerning which ship would lead following the exercise.

7. The exceptions were *Nelson* and *Revenge*. Although the former had an aircraft handling crane installed, no catapult was actually fitted.

8. It is not known whether this crane was actually fitted; if it was, it was swiftly removed again.

9. *Hood*'s football team had also played a team from *Graf Spee* during this period. For the record, the British team won 4–1.

9. *Royal Oak* was the only ship of this class to be so upgraded.

10. Why two single 5.5in guns were considered more useful than six 4in guns is not entirely clear, although of course the issue may have been ammunition stowage.

Chapter 4

1. Gensoul was senior to Vice-Admiral Whitworth, aboard *Hood*, and so commanded the joint operation.

2. With unfortunate consequences—see Chapter 6.

3. According to a report in *The Times*, the relevant clause in the Armistice ran as follows: 'The French Fleet, except that part left free for the safeguard of the French interests in the Colonial Empire, shall be collected in ports to be specified, demobilized and disarmed under German or Italian control. The German Government solemnly declare that they have no intention of using for their own purposes during the war the French Fleet stationed in ports under German control except those units necessary for coast surveillance and minesweeping. Except for that part of the Fleet destined for protection of Colonial interests, all ships outside French territorial waters must be recalled to France.' (*The Times*, 24 June 1940)

4. This last point is interesting: clearly, official thinking was that the war would be short-lived. It could of course not be foreseen at that time that it would expand into a global conflict.

5. Gensoul, aboard *Dunkerque*, had of course commanded the Franco-British force (which included *Hood*) that attempted to intercept the German battlecruisers *Scharnhorst* and *Gneisenau* the previous November (q.v.).

6. The fourth option—that of scuttling the ships—was not, apparently offered. However, when German forces occupied Toulon, the principal French naval base in the Mediterranean, in November 1942 this is precisely what happened.

7. A ship is said to have been straddled if enemy projectiles from one salvo or broadside fall both over and short of her, i.e. they are correct for bearing but not quite for range. The functional complement is bracketing, when shells fall either side of the target though are correct for range.

8. There was a postscript to this incident: within twenty-four hours *Rigault de Genouilly* had been sunk by the submarine *Pandora*, part of a patrol stationed to the east of Oran.

9. Possibly Somerville's distaste for the entire episode—which he did not hide from his superiors—had something to do with it.

10. Believed to be a record distance for a battleship not employing gunnery radar.

11. Paravanes, carried by all major warships, were torpedo-like devices streamed on either side of the bows by means of hawsers. They were equipped with fins to keep the equipment at a safe distance from the hull while being towed and a cutter for disengaging the mooring cable. The paravane, designed by a team led by Commander Sir Dennistoun Burney, first made its appearance during the First World War.

Chapter 5

1. This change of designation was symbolic: previously the German Navy had been known as the *Reichsmarine*, but now it had bellicose overtones.

2. It had long been the practice in the German Navy to identify new capital ships in terms of the individual vessels they were supposed to supplant (*Ersatz* = 'Replacement'); *Hannover* was one of the pre-dreadnoughts left over from the First World War.

3. Although with a length of 248m (813ft 8in) overall she was not the longest.

4. The institution of the convoy system was Lloyd George's 'most decisive achievement of the war.' (Taylor, p. 85)

5. For reasons which are unclear, *Bismarck* did not take on extra fuel whilst in Grimstadtfjord, although *Prinz Eugen* did.

6. A cable is one-tenth of a nautical mile, or 608ft. Therefore *Prince of Wales* was just over 800yds distant from *Hood*.

7. There is confusion here: some sources indicate that Holland received the 1922 signal in his flagship, others that he did know the true situation until a 2002 report, and still others that he was not aware of the positive identification until 2032, when *Norfolk* sent a report that she was being engaged. In any event, there were problems with *Suffolk*'s W/T equipment, either because of damp or because of icing.

8. Some authorities have suggested that an interception could have been made by about 0100 or 0200 on the 24th, i.e. some five hours after Holland received *Norfolk*'s report. This misconception appears to be based on the assumption that the two forces were sailing on directly opposing courses—which they were not.

9. Although it was not until much later in the war that radar equipment with a range of even half that at which Holland found himself from the enemy ships went into service, Holland was perhaps anxious about unknown enemy 'eavesdroppers'. *Bismarck* had a radar warning receiver, and it was thought that *Prinz Eugen* possibly had one too. The capabilities of these systems were unknown to Holland.

10. This seems to be the first occasion on which *Bismarck*'s companion was identified by name by the British. However, because of Holland's ban on wireless transmissions, Wake-Walker, aboard *Norfolk*, was never aware of his superior's intentions.

11. Which latter strategy would have required *Prince of Wales* to stop in order to hoist the Walrus aboard—something which Holland could not afford to do.

12. At these latitudes, in May, the skies even in the early hours of the morning are light.

13. *Prinz Eugen* was in the van because *Bismarck*'s radar had become unserviceable on account of blast damage from her own gunfire during the brief action with *Norfolk* the previous evening.

14. Some men apparently took cover in 'the aircraft hangar' (Coles/Briggs, p. 219). *Hood* of course had no facilities for handling aircraft at that time, and it is probable that the term was a crew nickname for the covered open area on the shelter deck at the base of the bridge superstructure

15. This, probably, is partially explained by the fact that *Prince of Wales* mounted six guns forward as against *Hood*'s four, and partially by the inherently more rapid rate of fire of her much more modern artillery. However, one of *Prince of Wales*'s guns broke down shortly after the action began. Salvos are fired when a number of guns—but not all—are discharged simultaneously; in Royal Navy practice, this generally meant two barrels at a time. *Bismarck*, firing from all four of her main turrets, was reported to be making four-gun salvos.

Chapter 6

1. Some German sources claim that *Bismarck* scuttled herself by having her sea cocks opened.

2. As far back as September 1918 the Director of Naval Construction, Sir Eustace Tennyson

d'Eyncourt, had warned of this very danger: he feared that if these warheads exploded, the ship would be cut in half. However, his observations, although considered, were ultimately ignored.

3. In fact, the muzzle velocity of *Bismarck*'s 38cm shells was 820ms, or 2,690fs.

4. German heavy shells at this time did feature exceptionally inert fuses: designers were anxious to avoid premature detonation on the surface of the enemy's armour, as had happened at Jutland.

5. Another recommendation made post-Jutland was that hand-loaded guns should have their ready-use ammunition stored in 1in thick steel lockers, and of course one of the consequences of this decision revealed itself during *Hood*'s final action.

6. German battleships and heavy cruisers had very similar superstructures and funnels—a deliberate design feature incorporated for the very purpose of confusing the enemy in his identification.

Epilogue

1. Funding for the expedition would be provided by Channel 4 Television.

2. Strict rules were followed for the expedition, the most important of which was that the wreck, if found, might be studied and photographed, but in no way disturbed.

BIBLIOGRAPHY

OFFICIAL RECORDS

ADM 1/9209: Battle Cruisers: Design (1916)

ADM 1/9210: Hood class: Armour and deck protection (1916)

ADM 1/11726: Loss of Hood in action with German battleship Bismarck: Report of Board of Inquiry

ADM 1/30817: Loss of HMS Hood

ADM 116/4351–2: Loss of HMS Hood in action with German battleship Bismarck: Boards of Inquiry

ADM 156/107: Collision between HM Ships Hood and Renown

ADM 178/110: Invergordon Mutiny: Narrative of events by R. A. Tomkinson, SO Atlantic Fleet

ADM 186/249: 15″ Mark II mountings, HMS Hood

ADM 186/797: Operations against French Fleet at Mers-el-Kebir, 3–6 July 1940

ADM 199/1187–8: Pursuit and destruction of German battleship Bismarck

ADM 202/422: Operation "Primrose": Operations by Royal Marines in Norway, 1940

ADM 226/20: Battle cruiser design 1915–16: Complete report (1917)

ADM 226/23: HMS Hood: Analysis of results of speed trials

ADM 226/24: HMS Hood: Results of shallow-water trials

ADM 234/317: Operations against French Fleet at Mers-el-Kebir, 3–6 July 1940

ADM 234/321–2: Chase and sinking of German battleship Bismarck, 23–27 May 1941

ADM 267/64: Hood: Board of Inquiry into loss

BOOKS AND ARTICLES

Bradford, Ernle, *The Mighty Hood*, Hodder & Stoughton (London, 1959)

Brown, D. K., *Nelson to Vanguard: Warship Design and Development, 1923 to 1945*, Chatham Publishing (London, 2000)

Brown, D. K., *The Grand Fleet: Warship Design and Development, 1906 to 1922*, Conway Maritime Press (London, 1999)

Burt, R. A., *British Battleships 1919–1939*, Arms & Armour Press (London, 1993)

Campbell, N. J. M, *Battlecruisers* ('*Warship* Special'), Conway Maritime Press (London, 1978)

Chesneau, Roger (ed.), *Conway's All the World's Fighting Ships, 1922–1946*, Conway Maritime Press (London, 1980)

Churchill, W. S., *The Second World War*, Vols 1 and 2, Cassell & Co (London, 1948 and 1951)

Coles, Alan, *Invergordon Scapegoat: The Betrayal of Admiral Tomkinson*, Sutton Publishing (Stroud, 1993)

Coles, Alan, and Briggs, Ted, *Flagship Hood: The Fate of Britain's Mightiest Warship*, Robert Hale (London, 1996)

Jellicoe of Scapa, Admiral Viscount, *The Grand Fleet 1914–16: Its Creation, Development and Work*, Cassell & Co (London, 1919)

Jurens, W. J., 'The Loss of HMS Hood: A Re-Examination', *Warship International*, No 2, 1987, International Naval Research Organization (Toledo, 1987)

Kennedy, Ludovic, *Pursuit: The Chase and Sinking of the Bismarck*, Collins (London, 1974)

Marder, Arthur J., *From the Dardanelles to Oran: Studies of the Royal Navy in War and Peace, 1915–1940*, Oxford University Press (Oxford, 1974)

Mearns, David, and White, Rob, *Hood and Bismarck The Deep-Sea Discovery of an Epic Battle*, Channel 4 Books (London, 2001)

Müllenheim-Rechberg, Baron Burkard von, *Battleship Bismarck: A Survivor's Story*, The Bodley Head (London, 1980)

Northcott, Maurice, *Hood: Design and Construction* ('Ensign' series), Bivouac Books (1975)

O'Connor, V. C. Scott, *The Empire Cruise*, Riddle, Smith & Duffus (1925)

Parkes, Oscar, *British Battleships 1860–1950*, Seeley, Service & Co (London, 1957)

Preston, Antony, *Battleships of World War I*, Arms and Armour Press (London, 1972)

Raven, Alan, *King George the Fifth Class Battleships* ('Ensign' series), Bivouac Books (1972)

Raven, Alan, and Roberts, John, *British Battleships of World War Two : The Development and Technical History of the Royal Navy's Battleships and Battlecruisers from 1911 to 1946*, Arms & Armour Press (London, 1977)

Rhys-Jones, Graham, *The Loss of the Bismarck: An Avoidable Disaster*, Cassell & Co (London, 1999)

Roberts, John, *Battlecruisers*, ('Shipshape' series), Chatham Publishing (London, 1998)

———, *The Battlecruiser Hood* ('Anatomy of the Ship' series), Conway Maritime Press (London, 1982)

Robertson, R. G., *HMS Hood: Battle-Cruiser 1916–1941* ('Warship Profile' series), Profile Publications (Windsor, 1972)

Roskill, Stephen, *Naval Policy Between the Wars*, 2 vols, Collins (London, 1976)

———, *The Navy at War*, 1939–1945, Collins (London, 1960)

———, *The War at Sea*, Vol. 1, HMSO (London, 1954)

Schmalenbach, Paul, *KM Bismarck* ('Warship Profile' series), Profile Publications (Windsor, 1972)

Tarrant, V. E., *King George V Class Battleships*, Arms & Armour Press (London, 1991)

Taverner, Nixie, *Hood's Legacy*, Bernard Durnford Publishing (Bramber, 2001)

Taylor, A. J. P., *English History 1914–1945* ('The Oxford History of England' series), Oxford University Press (Oxford, 1965)

Weldon, D. G., 'H.M.S. Hood', *Warship International*, No 2, 1972, International Naval Research Organization (Toledo, 1972)

Winklareth, Robert J., *The Bismarck Chase: New Light on a Famous Engagement*, Chatham Publishing (London, 1998)

WEB SITES

There are innumerable websites dealing with the design and history of HMS *Hood*, some very basic, some very good. At the time of writing, the three most significant are:

www.hmshood.com This is a quite outstanding site, providing an enormous amount of information, pleasingly presented, covering the ship herself, the crew, memorabilia and reference materials; there is also a forum and a message board. One of the projects currently underway is the collection of photographs and information relating to men lost with the ship. The site is also 'home' to the HMS Hood Association, membership details of which can be found within it.

www.channel4.com/hood Another excellent site, concentrating on the search for the wreck of HMS *Hood* that took place in July 2001. Highlights include a 15-minute video download of Magellan 725's investigation of the remains.

www.warships1.com/W-INRO/INRO_Hood _p1, _p2, _p3 and _p4 This reproduces Bill Jurens' excellent article on the loss of *Hood* referred to above.

www.warships1.com/GERbb08_Bismarck_ history.htm A site which gives a good account of Operation 'Rheinübung', with detailed maps and a selection of photographs.

INDEX